BREAKIN

BREAKING BOB

BREAKING BOB

Anthony Pillage

Breaking Bob

First published in 2016 in the UK

3P Publishing Ltd
C E C, London Road
Corby
NN17 5EU

A catalogue number for this book is available from the British Library

ISBN 978-1-911559-10-8

Cover design: Sarah Pillage

To Bob. Thanks for the memories. But I won. Just,

Contents

bob₄

pronoun BRITISH # bob₁

verb

verb: **bob**; 3rd person present: **bobs**; past tense: **bobbed**;
past participle: **bobbed**; gerund or present participle:
bobbing

1 **1.**   Make a quick, short movement up and down. "I could
see his head bobbing about"

bob₂

noun: **bob**; plural noun: **bobs**

1 **1.**   a style in which the hair is cut short and evenly all
round so that it hangs above the shoulders. "she wore
her hair in a fashionable bob"

bob₃

noun BRITISH *informal*

noun: **bob**; plural noun: **bob**

1 **1.** An annoying cancer, genus Thymic Carcinoma, dormant
for the time being
Complete wanker.

Explaining Bob

Before I start this literary journey, I feel it's only proper to introduce the now-legendary Thymic Carcinoma known colloquially as "Bob".

Bob has been a part of my life for the best part of two years now and has provided some of the most life changing experiences imaginable....... the little fucker that he is! Bob is now gone, for at least the time being. I can't say I miss him particularly but I can certainly thank him for helping mould me into the incarnation that I am today.

"Bob" though needs to be explained. I was diagnosed with cancer just after one of my heroes; the wonderful Rik Mayall had tragically died. Out of all his many superb characters, the Lord Flashheart one had always stood out loud and extremely fucking proud to me. I bloody adored him and oft quoted him as one of my role models. If you recall his stunning entry in series two of *Blackadder* (the Elizabethan one) all thrusting and roguishly handsome, he personified so much of whom I aspired to be. The episode culminates with him resoundingly woofing at all and sundry before making off with Edmunds' intended bride "Bob". One can only imagine what many unspeakable things he was going to do to her and certainly seemed to have plans to fuck her right royally, exactly what I intended to do with my cancer, hence Bob.

I know the beautiful Lisa Lynch of the C Word Book and the Cancer Blog *A Right Tit* called hers *The Bullshit*, as she couldn't bear to use the word cancer. It's a sort of Voldermort, he who must not be named-type scenario. We all deal with this in our own ways I guess!!

Just please remember though the Flashheart WOOF, as it will provide the end piece of this book, with me in the legendary musician, and cancer survivor, Wilko Johnson's dressing room as well as popping up at random times throughout the narrative. The woof almost became my catchphrase on social media, even to the point where I had it tattooed on my arm to always remember the importance of the fight I was engaging in. Even two years down the line, many of my friends still greet me with it. So put your hands on your hips and gird your loins my darlings, we are in for a bumpy ride of that I promise you. WOOF!!

BREAKING BOB

I have used Billy Connolly's adage that any decent book must have a minimum of seventy-six fucks in it, so please if you are easily offended put this down right now.

Breaking Bob

People ask me where the title of the book comes from and, of course, it's from the now huge cult TV series, *Breaking Bad,* starring the wonderful character of Walter White, a chemist who is diagnosed with terminal cancer and sets off on a wild journey of self-discovery making met-amphetamine to support his family for the time when he is deceased. The irony is I used the title even before I could watch the series as it was a little too close to my heart at the time.

However, let me take a moment to explain the format of this book. As those of you who follow me will be aware, I have been on Facebook for many years and have built up a substantial following over that time, mainly for my martial arts. (Obviously if this is the first time we have met please feel free to add me to your cluster of friends). What started as me just sharing information regarding my illness, soon built into a major part of my life for the following eighteen months.

I couldn't believe just what a cathartic process it was, sharing all the ups and downs of my illness, until I had time to take stock and re-read the posts then the enormity of what had happened really hit me. At times social media was my only portal into the outside world. You see, if you haven't been confined to a hospital bed you would not probably understand my next words exactly. The day before my operation I could have basically gone anywhere and done more or less anything, anywhere, in the world. Then ka-fucking-boom your entire universe is restricted to the size of a hospital bed and then down to your five inch iPhone screen, which then became my only window to the great outside. Through social media and especially Facebook, the love and support I got from my many friends and followers kept me sane during the really bad times and managed to nourish me emotionally and spiritually; keeping me going when I really thought I couldn't take anymore. I cannot thank everyone enough who was part of that journey.

Then I had this bloody great EUREKA moment...why not do a book based on my Facebook posts over the past eighteen months? How unique that would be?

Then I realized that's called a diary!! Doh.... yet another complete disappointment. I wasn't the literary trailblazer I had taken myself as being. However, as life ebbed on, this project started to take a life of its own. What was initially going to be the journal of the Facebook Year, I realized it needed a lot more in depth of explanation and, most certainly, soul baring about the entire journey, as I had learned so much about myself and about cancer over the past two years. The book may have more merit than I at first had given it credence. So here I am sitting in the middle of a forest in North Wales, actually putting quill to parchment, metaphorically, and having stopped the bloody procrastination I am so often accusing others of. I am getting this bad-boy underway. I am truthfully looking towards Samuel L Jackson playing me in the forthcoming biopic!! Now that would be more than interesting.

Misquoted in *Pulp Fiction,* but my thoughts nonetheless:

Ezekial 24: 15 to 17
15 "Thus says the Lord God: Because the Philistines acted revengefully and took vengeance with malice of soul to destroy in never-ending enmity, 16 therefore thus says the Lord God, Behold, I will stretch out my hand against the Philistines, and I will cut off the Cherethites and destroy the rest of the seacoast. 17 I will execute great vengeance on them with wrathful rebukes. Then they will know that I am the Lord, when I lay my vengeance upon them."

Again my thoughts about smiting Bob in any way, shape or form that I could came to the fore, but I always thought the follow up part of Julius's speech from *Pulp Fiction* was equally as important; the part where he talks about changing and how aspects of life change you.

And that my friend sums up the change or evolution you get from overcoming this hideous disease. It bloody alters the very fabric of who you are. Fact. I know I'm a far better person and a far happier person having gone through this whole process.

Basically you will see the FB posts forming the spine of the book. I will be adding the flesh around it by sharing my thoughts from the time at a deeper and far more in-depth level, hopefully sharing the knowledge I have accrued during these times to help others facing similar battles. My thoughts have resoundingly changed over the past year on life, the universe and basically just about fucking everything. This is a good thing. Cancer has a habit of making you evolve and is that old adage true "what doesn't kill us makes us stronger"? I think so, but maybe as well "what doesn't evolve in nature will eventually die". I certainly think if I hadn't evolved, I would be as John Cleese once eloquently said, '*pining for the fucking*

13

fjords, this Pillage is no more he has ceased to be, he's shuffled off this mortal coil and joined the choir invisible !!!!!'

As a recent quote from a stage 4 cancer sufferer said on a BBC programme *The Big C and Me "when you are told the diagnosis you literally die there and then on the spot only to be reborn".* This is exactly what happens when given the diagnosis we all fear and for someone like me, having been given a second chance, it was imperative to take the bull proverbially by the horns and as Robin Williams said in the wonderful film *Dead Poets Society.*

"Carpe diem. Seize the day."

Was I scared? Of course I was. Did it trouble me? Of course it did. However, in the whole of the following twenty-four months I am extremely proud to say I only let it affect me badly on twelve days out of the seven hundred or so that I was engaged in the conflict. Twelve days of the most mind blowing, abject misery, which was literally, the worst I have ever felt in my entire life, but the reality is it was only a handful. This is where the power of the martial arts and the mindset it engenders really came into its own. The mental fortitude developed over the preceding fifteen years was the foundation that saw me through, of that there is very little doubt whatsofuckingever.

But I would also wholeheartedly ascribe to Walt Whitman's words (who was also quoted in the same film) 'O *me! O life! Of the questions of these recurring; of the endless trains of the faithless... of cities filled with the foolish; what good amid these, O me, O life?'* Answer. *That you are here — that life exists, and identity; that the powerful play goes on and you may contribute*

14

*a verse. That the powerful play goes on and you may contribute
a verse. What will your verse be?"*

In other words what will be your contribution to the world?
What part will you take? As Paulo Coelho alludes in the
wonderful book *The Alchemist* you need to find what your
personal legend really is. I always thought that it was helping
people through teaching martial arts, but as I am writing this at
the beginning of October 2016 I currently have eleven people I
am supporting with their own battles with cancer. I am proud
of that fact and I am sure many more will follow. This is my
verse at least for the time being.

So as you can already see I am Carpe Diem-ing like a fucking
madman!

Cancer Bloody Cancer

People get shocked when I tell them "I'm really glad I have cancer". You get that what the fuck just happened look on their faces until you explain. But the reality is that over the past eighteen months, I have had some of the most remarkable things happen to me that would never have come about without this bloody illness raising its head. It has helped me become a far better person and enjoy life at an intensity that very few could match. After speaking to other survivors this is not an uncommon occurrence. So the genuine heartfelt truth is I am 100% glad I have gone through this and of course with the proviso that I have come out the other end scarred, bloody but still smiling.

My own dealings previously with the dreaded C word have been singularly unpleasant as I am sure it is of most people. As a young man of seventeen, I watched my beloved grandfather die from what started as prostate cancer but sadly spread throughout his body. The term riddled was used often by the family and medical teams to describe his illness. I was with him when he passed, as I was with my Mum, who beat breast cancer the first time around, but succumbed when it hit her again four years later. My uncle Ted (Mum's brother) died of lung cancer when I was in my twenties. We are a family where it seems to be our fate to have this awful thing beat the crap out of us.

So as a heavy smoker I thought that whatever I did to myself I was predestined to die of the BIG C. The irony is that my particular Thymic Carcinoma can strike whether you smoke or not, he's a random little shit. It's a rare and particularly aggressive one, seen only about four times a year at the Arden Cancer Centre in Coventry. Of this I was pleased...I'd hate to have an illness that was a frigging pussy!! There was probably little I could have done to prevent it. You see when that spectre is hanging over you there was rarely a day when I didn't think of dying of it. It's like the playground bully hiding in the shadows, the one that terrifies you but won't stand in front of you and fight. The sad irony being is that stress made me smoke even more. So when I got the first indications there may be something wrong with me, I truthfully wasn't surprised. I clearly remember talking to my dear mate Ian Goehler in about March of 2014 saying I knew there was something seriously wrong with me but had no idea as to what. As a typical bloke it took nearly six months before I went to the doctors with a cough, which ironically had nothing to do with the cancer. So lesson number one chaps: GO TO THE BLOODY doctor! Stop being stoic and swallow that machismo. If I hadn't had my diagnosis at that time then I would be dead by now, of that I have little doubt.

Remember your body and brains are pretty much on your side. If something feels wrong it probably is!

In August I was a passenger in Sarah, my wife's car, when it was sideswiped whilst going round a roundabout. It wasn't a bad crash by any means, but I had been bending down picking up a piece of paper I had dropped. This meant that at the point of impact my spine was twisted. I ended up going to have physiotherapy sessions at the Nuffield Hospital in Leamington Spa. Over the coming months I gradually noticed I was getting pain in my chest. The lovely Bethan, my therapist, felt it was referred pain from my back and neck. The pain got worse and worse but I felt happy with her prognosis.

I then developed a particularly nasty and troublesome cough and toddled off to my doctors to get some antibiotics. My normal physician, Dr Fullbrook, wasn't available so I came across Dr Tom Harper for the first time. He didn't see unduly concerned, but given my smoking history thought it prudent to get a chest X-ray, as there was a small crackle on my right lung. This was on the Monday (7th October). He told me that I wouldn't get any results for at least 7-10 days so the following morning I went to the Radiology Dept. at the Heathcote Hospital in lovely Leamington Spa where the nurse also happily quoted I would hear back in about 7-10 days.

Then on Thursday evening (only two days later) I finished teaching, checked my phone and noticed I had three missed calls from the doctors. I, of course, realized that potentially this was catastrophic news. He wasn't likely to have called to say "Oh well done Mr. Pillage you are tickety fucking boo. Let's go for a beer and a sausage supper at Mrs. Miggins Pie Emporium". I still remember vividly the feeling of abject despair and the icy tendril of utter fear that stabbed me through my stomach. But the time was 8.00pm and the surgery was closed (although I tried to call just to get some information, knowing full well they would be shut, that's how desperate I was). I think that night, in many respects, was the worst of the whole journey. I was petrified beyond anything I could ever have imagined. Was I riddled with cancer? Was I going to be dead by Xma? All night the demons visited my poor battered brain and gave little respite. At 8am I was on the phone to see if I could glean any further information. "The doctor will call you back as soon as he is free," said the obviously harassed receptionist. The next hour consisted of me checking my phone every six seconds in case I missed his call. I remember calling my friend and mentor, Steve Rowe, just to talk to someone as I felt I was going to burst. The doctors' number flashed up but I was too late to get it. Aggggghhhhhhhhhh! I called back within a heartbeat. "Sorry Dr Harper's line is busy ...can I take a message?" ARGGHHHHHHH! No you can't ......shit shit shit. Within a minute he had called back though. If he hadn't I would have had a bloody coronary!

"Mr. Pillage I'm really sorry the X-ray seems to have picked up an anomaly, we are going to need to get you checked as quickly as possible." Although in truth I knew that the news wasn't going to be great, it still hit me like a train. A fucking huge train with spiky bits KABOOOOOOOOOM. I put the phone down and felt the blood drain from my body. That's it. It's over.

Little did I know then that the reality would be that Bob was going to change my life forever and was perhaps the greatest thing that ever happened to me. Just how fucked up is that, eh?

In truth I should have looked to my own history. My life had altered fourteen years previously when I had a Deep Vein Thrombosis (DVT), which had caused a pulmonary embolism in my left lung. It nearly killed me and I was in the Walsgrave Hospital for the best part of six weeks. During that time I had spent a lot of my waking hours thinking about what would have happened if I had died? What legacy would I have left? Who would have missed me? The sad truth was nothing and very few. Sobering thoughts. I had always been a keen sportsman, playing a good standard of rugby, squash and, in fact, most sports. Sadly I had been involved in a nasty car accident some years before when a low loader lorry had hit my stationary car at about 50 mph, causing severe problems to my neck and upper spine. So I just stopped all sport, did nothing and just vegetated. This may have been the reason for the DVT. We will never know.

However, fate played an interesting hand only a few days after being discharged from hospital. A man called Barry knocked on my door asking would anyone at the house be interested in starting some karate. I had done various martial arts as a child and young man and the thought appealed to me. Was this a sign? In hindsight…. absobloodylutely. So the following Wednesday I walked round to St Augustine's Church Hall in my shiny new gi (karate suit) and there started my martial arts life, a journey which would culminate in becoming a nationally known martial arts instructor and travelling the world teaching Pressure Point seminars. So the reality is the fat woman hadn't even started warming her pendulous throat yet. The DVT had transpired to be the best thing to happen to me…surely Cancer couldn't ever in a million years have that sort of outcome? Well yes my friends it has and in ways one could never ever, ever envisage.

N.B. The Facebook posts that are listed below are pertinent to the cancer and are an unedited account of the whole of the following eighteen months or so. I have deliberately not changed the punctuation as I feel it needs to be read as it spewed forth from my somewhat deranged brain…a sort of stream of consciousness style of writing maybe. My deeper thoughts that have been added in italics offer perhaps some insight into what was going on at the time and have been written subsequently.

I would like to hope that this book inspires, motivates and gives encouragement to its readers or family and friends who may be suffering from cancer. I will warn you now and I have debated this point for a while now. There is a section of about twenty pages at around the time of the radiotherapy where I felt very ill and literally everyday was a struggle or I felt a new ailment had hit me. There is little humour or insight in this dark period and it may be hard to read as I had literally nothing left in the tank whatsoever mentally. I decided to leave this in as although it may be a little tedious to plough through, it is exactly how my spirits and mind were. The thing is I can't even remember anything from this time apart from feeling lousy and watching television at home. Nothing whatsobloodyever. It was as if time had just stood still, then you are reborn at the end of the process.

Bob Appears

Facebook – the diary begins:

October 11 2014

I've had so many private messages on here and bits that I'll just put this up quickly. After having a chest X-ray on Tuesday the Doc has informed me that there is an anomaly in my lung. They are fast tracking me through for further tests. Being a long time smoker I am naturally expecting the worst. HOWEVER, I will fight whatever this is all the way.... I is Pillagius Maximus and I will fucking roaaaarrrrrrrrrrr

So that was the very first post regarding the cancer. As I mentioned earlier I am wiser than I was then. Roaaaaaarrrrrrrrrrrrr Jesus H Christ. I could hardly whip up a whimper if truth be told.

October 15 2014

Hospital appointment 9am next Wednesday now..........bring it on bitches!!

The hospital had moved quickly and then some, this concerned the hell out of me.

I travelled to Glastonbury on the Sunday with a friend. We walked up the tor, went to Chalice Well and listened to a blues band in a beautiful old pub until late. I love the whole energy from this part of the world and it did me the world of good to just stop thinking about the bloody illness. I will always remember this day with unique fondness as it was going to be the last really happy day for over a year.

October 21 2014
Tomorrow at 9.00am I go to the Warwick Hospital and if I am honest whatever they throw at me I am ready to deal with. Just wanting to find out what is wrong so I can get better asap, ready to enjoy the next and wondrous part of my life.....its safe to say that already this whole thing has changed my world. No cigs, no sugar, vegan diet, new outlook on life. But I will beat this. I think it's time for me to break and evolve again, that's my gut feeling. (*How true was this statement looking back, see listen to your gut it is so often right !!)*

I look at this post and smile. The belligerent and never quitting side of my nature is already kicking in. I had stopped smoking the previous Friday after the doctor's phone call. That's after thirty- five years of being a nicotine junkie. It's amazing what abject fear can make you achieve. So in less than a week I had already done more research and taken steps on how to help heal/help myself than I had done during the past fifty odd years. How right I was and how much do I have to thank all the many friends who had pointed me towards the holistic path. Namaste, you beautiful motherfuckers!! Without your input, god knows where this story would have ended.

It was about this time I took a phone call from Will Henshaw, a great friend of mine who had beaten lung cancer a few years earlier. Will is famous for the BBC programme Mind Body and Kickass Moves. *As ever he was the gentleman and offered sage council. He did however ask, "Was I having night sweats?" as they are a pretty good indicator that cancer is present. Sadly for the previous month I had literally had to change my bed twice a*

23

night as I was sweating so profusely. Bum, so it probably wasn't the flu or male menopause then as I had perhaps thought.
But I had already started reading up on what to do to help myself. This is why I believe I am still here today. Sheer fucking belligerence and a self - belief that far outweighed my fear.

October 22 2014
Well as I thought. Shadow in lung right hand side quite a lot bigger than I hoped.
In hospital next Tuesday for CT scan and they will do a bronchoscopy and remove tissue samples
Apparently I'll be out of it for a day or so
No change there then
Thank you all for the hundreds of beautiful messages and love
Namaste

You see the tumour (Bob) was in fact so large it was showing clearly through a lung x-ray. I had spoken to a friend just after this news had been delivered who was unaware of my plight. He had been looking at holistic treatments for some time and had become a huge advocate of the Phoenix Tears movement started by Rick Simpson in America, where cannabis oil had had near on miraculous outcomes on people with not only cancer but a whole host of other pernicious diseases as well. The following day he left work at 5.30 pm, drove over 200 miles to arrive at my door with a bag of cannabis tablets he had secured for me. I will never forget this great kindness and how much I appreciated his concern. For obvious reasons I cannot name him but I will call him Maverick!

October 27 2014
Oh dear tomorrow has come round quicker than I could have ever imagined......... I may be out of it for a while. Many thanks

for all the messages of love and support as well as the people coming into the dojo. Whatever they find, I am 100% prepared honestly I think. But I will fight it with every cell of my body. I have an awful lot to live for and who else will be as big, butch and Pope Fabulousy as me !!
One love people xx

Today was also the day when I was awarded the cancer card...yes a big laminated C that I carried about on my person for a few weeks until the joke wore a little thin. So basically when I didn't want to do something I just pulled out the C card and people wouldn't make me do it...bloody marvellous !! This is where Sarah really came into her own. She wouldn't let me mope and helped made me laugh when there was no laughter to be had. The C card was a stroke of utter genius.

For your interest Pope Fabulous is the name of my video company and another Pillage alter Ego. I also have Simon the autistic savant and Rod the Welsh drunkard. So be warned.

October 28 2014
Complete cock up this morning. Get there massively early to the Warwick Hospital Endoscopy unit (where the letter says to go). Tell the lady I need a CT scan first (according to the letter). Wait an hour. Get wheeled into what looks like a operating theatre. *"Where's your scan Mr. Pillage"? I haven't had it says I.* "You'll have to come back next week" says they. Ok says I. So I have to go through the same thing again in a week's time Agggghhhhh.

So let's elaborate on this. I ended up getting to the Hospital at 7.15am absolutely shitting oneself. Go into the Endoscopy unit and register. You see in my mind I was going to go into a nice little room where a pleasant doctor and his pretty young nurse would be waiting with a cup of tea and a smile. I didn't realize for one minute that they were sending me in a FULL BLOWN operating theatre type room with eight people in it all gowned and masked up. This bloody scared the shite out of me and although loins were truly girded, the fact that they had made a mistake and had to potentially go through all of this again filled me with the deepest of dread.

October 30 2014
This mental limbo with the hospital is doing my bloody head in aghhhhhh

November 3 2014
Well start week four as a raw vegan non smoker .... although I may have cheated on a couple of occasions with a piece of chicken. Smoking stop is easy and although I felt that smoking in some ways had defined and limited me I rarely have had urges to start again.

Just getting prepared for tomorrow's biopsy. Starting to get a little nervous if honest now I have an idea as to what they will be doing.

November 4 2014
This morning I have been blessed by literally hundreds of messages of support and love
Many from complete strangers
I am truly astounded and grateful beyond words
Thank you
Namaste xx
Well I'm canularred up (is there such a word .. don't give a shit though if there isn't)
Ready to go to theatre
It's lala time for Pillagius
I hope I'm not improper when then stick things inside my lung
xx
See you all soon
(I see you know your endoscopy well) If you need a smile look up GET YOUR HANDS OFF MY PENIS on YouTube. Then this will make some sense. If not no worries its bloody hilarious on its own merits !
Sadly once again this procedure never happened. But the CAT scan did.
Yes my friends they cocked up massively again ……. but they did the CAT scan which broke the news rather suddenly.
Not great news sadly
Seems I have a malignant cancer in my pericardium
Bit in shock
But at least my lungs are OK
This would at least explain my breathlessness and chest pains

OK MF's let put some clarity on this. My "wonderful" doctor ... let's call him THUNDERTWONK McTWATFACE, without any biopsy results, tells me I have one of the worst forms of cancer. I of course (as my mates also did) went home and looked this one up. Google doctoring never the best idea, eh chaps? NOT A GREAT one. Be dead in months. I will never ever forgive this man and his unnecessary and wrong diagnosis. Unforgivable, as this mentally knocked whatever stuffing I had left out of me. The worst bit of doctoring in this whole tale. I hope he never has to have a similar prognosis. I am a generous God but would have willingly punched him repeatedly in the throat for many hours or made him go to a Guy Bloom seminar (only joking Guy xx).

It took me two months to shake off the feeling of hopelessness he created with his misdiagnosis.

Sarah couldn't attend this meeting, so my old mate Gavin made an excuse to come down from Liverpool to see me. I have no words to describe him. He is my spiritual brother certainly, great martial artist certainly, hard as nails bloke undoubtedly. I walked out of THUNDERTWONKS office numb and reeling. "How did you get on bud?" enquired the big fella. I remember just looking at him, unable to speak with tears welling up in my eyes. He realized just how severe things were and started welling up himself. We looked away and walked in abject silence back to the car. No words were needed so we just hugged for a minute. A beautiful moment I believe only men could share. We never spoke of it again.

A message from my friend helped an awful lot though. A man who little did we know at that time then would be publishing this book.

Andy Gibney
So, today you had a bad day. In time you will cry, swear, stamp your feet and feel utterly shit, but remember the mark you have made on all of us, those who call you 'friend'. Three years ago you helped me through a very, very rough time. Your kindness has always stayed with me. All the phone calls we have had, the crazy YouTube clips, introducing the UK to Master Ken, SENI, Richard Bustillo seminars and meals at Cosmo, philosophical discussions and stories to curl the hair of any well behaved person. I am glad you are my friend. I am sorry to hear of your bad news, but I have no doubts that you will fight and live and prevail, although how that will turn out we'll leave to Derek Accorah and the psychics. What I am certain of is that you make my life a happier place and I look forward to seeing you upset people, make others laugh and continue inspiring me and all of those who love you like we do, for a very long time to come yet.

November 5 2014
Morning all
I am overwhelmed by all your messages, text's, calls and carrier pigeons sent over the past 24 hours. I hadn't realised just the seemingly profound affect I seem to have had on so many people's lives. Whatever happens to me that fact gives me the very deepest of comfort and joy. I am fine at the moment but know this is a battle I have to win.... so I will .... simples. So please keep these energy levels up for me to feed upon, being the energy slut that I am.

This was the time I realized just how powerful people's support was and what a deciding factor this was going to be in the following year. The need for energy would be paramount in my healing process. But more of that later.

29

November 6 2014
I am in a good place tonight
I have been visited by literally dozens of friends today
Showing support and love
Thank you all from the bottom of my heart for making the effort
I am humbled xx
Namaste

"I have no real discernible talent...apart from the ability to be me. And I'm getting better and better at that with every passing day."
Tony Pillage

Two of these meetings will stay with me for a very long time and were defining moments. In the morning I was feeling very, very down. The weight and enormity of what I was facing was pressing heavily and then the phone went. Mikey Wright and Eddie Quinn were coming to visit. We sat eating seeds and drinking green tea as I was heavily into this holistic diet path, (they tasted like shit btw). We sat there and laughed and laughed for the best part of two hours. My soul and spirits were lifted. One can never underestimate the feeling of having true and beautiful friends.

The second visit was a very different affair.

An old student Connor Lake came in with his friend Tyson Moranis, whose Mum had died of cancer the previous year (I know that Connor had been very close to her). They had felt the grief that the sickness brings. I ended up in tears and felt awful. Connor said something which I will never forget "Man, you can't go out like this. You are a warrior, I want you carried aloft on

shields when you die. That's how you need to be remembered".
Whether this was my ego listening or it just gave me the kick in
the bollocks I needed I never forgot this and it really honestly
helped a million fold. It was at this time I realized a very simple
truth. If I only had a while to live, I needed to live well and more
importantly die well. I could either sit there and mope or I could
engage in what I do best and go out with a memorable bang.
Total no brainer then lol

November 8 2014
Well I've had a lovely day in the company of Richard Barnes
and his wonderful family
Thank m you all so much for the time and courtesy
Had a blast
Feel quite good tonight
Thank all

November 10 2014
Does anyone know where I can get a Vitamin C injection in the
Coventry area please

I had just read Philip Day's book Cancer, why we are still dying
to know the truth. *MASSIVE doses of Vitamin C. Couldn't find*
where to get in anywhere until a year later when I visited the
awesome Breakspear Clinic in Hemel Hempstead. More of this
place later. However, if you have someone in your life with the
Cancer then buy this book I implore you. It is a wealth of
information. Info also at www.credence .org

November 11 2014
Shit just got real
Full body PET scan next week
It's scary time

November 12 2014
Down to 15 stone 5 lbs
Yuck
Just got out of the hospital
I have an aggressive tumour the size of a tennis ball in my chest that's pushing my heart out of the way
Looks like an op next week
It's time to fuck this bad boy off
I'm glad it's an aggressive tumour
I'd hate a quiet one!!
Onwards and upwards chaps

Will Garnsworthy
Right now my friend Anthony Pillage is battling, he has an aggressive tumour in his pericardium, this is the fight of his life.
Tony is unique, he makes Flashheart look like Justin Bieber!.
Tony hit the English martial arts scene like a torpedo, he threw away the rule book and went about it in a unique way. A way which put fun at the forefront and brought people together. He has had many, many challenges in the time that I have known him.
Tony taught me that you can have a right laugh while training in martial arts. I will never forget training at his on Joe Carslake's coaching course, the fun, the camaraderie with such a great group of people, getting zapped with his shock knife, the opening of his dojo in 2008 when a group of martial arts masters were chasing each other around a dojo on space hoppers in the early AM. Tony brought Master Ken to the UK, and hosted a Master Ken seminar with Royce Gracie looking on. He is not what you expect from a martial arts instructor, he is much more wonderful than most.

Wishing you the strength to overcome. Much love to ya big man

And this post was where the legend started. So thank you Mr. Garnsworthy for your eruditeness.

Well it looks like my last major event before I have my operation is going to be the MAI awards this Sunday. Frankly, I couldn't think of a place where I will have so many friends offering love and support to help me get through this. Thank you all so far..... namaste to all the wonderfully supportive people I have in my life

Hahaha little did we know that would pan out over the next year...watch this space! You see me use the word Namaste a lot and in truth it's my favourite word (well after moist, obviously).

The literal translation of this greeting varies with each language; however, they are all pretty much saying the same thing. In Sanskrit, the word 'namah' means bow, 'as' means I,, and 'te' means you, translating into "I bow to you." A Hindi friend once explained that Namaskar is translated from 'namoh' and 'sanskar' translating loosely into English as "I bow to godly/good qualities within you,' as her culture always tries to see the good in all things.

Some other popular translations and meanings of the word Namaste I hear frequently include:

> *The Divine light in me acknowledges the Divine light in you.*
> *The God in me greets and meets the God in you.*
> *I honor the spirit in you that is also in me.*

33

The Divine wisdom in me recognizes and acknowledges the Divine wisdom in you.

Regardless of the language you speak, the word simply invokes a sense of sharing a spiritual connection and creates a sense and feeling of oneness and balance. Essentially, it's a way that all humans can connect and I bloody love it.

November 13 2014

Motonari Budokai or Darren Hand as he is more often called:
My friend Anthony Pillage recently discovered that he has an "aggressive tumor" near his heart.

In times like this people need to be supportive, but knowing Tony, its hard to do it in a heartfelt "touchy feely" way... Lets face it, in our time in our dojo, we know cancer as it affected Paula, WE ALL supported her, so can the club members please do the same?

So in light if Tony's non touchy feeling nature.... I'm just going to list a few things, a few great memories I've had with Tony.

1: Him ringing me from the UK the EVENING before my 3rd Dan grading (even though we never met) to wish me luck, and him ringing me after to see how it went.

2: Him running a series of courses with my Sensei at the time to help him out, and to make sure things went ok.

3: Him organizing to have my Sensei's lifetime achievement award presented at SENI by none other than Royce Gracie.

4: At that event, making sure that all of our visitors were treated like royalty in an event in which THOUSANDS attended, including some notable celebrities.

5: The full Lipped kiss he welcomed me with in the Hotel the evening before. In front of several Hanshi grades! Remembering that that was our first actual meeting.

6: Him Flying over at his own expense to Ireland to spend time with my Sensei, as he was in a bad place needing a friend.

7: Him beating me up at a seminar the same weekend (he didn't come for the seminar, I asked the organisers to let him teach),

8: The fact that at Tommy Jordan's dojo he was welcomed with applause.

9: Him letting my daughter Aoibhín win a game of Ninja at the first Keepers Seminar, as, as he put it, "she is going to have a hard enough time living up to being your daughter, but not today!"

10: Him coming to Tullamore that night, and with the enthusiasm of a beginner chatting ALL night about Martial Arts and then proceeding to demonstrate techniques on Gary. A GREAT night.

11: Eating Kebabs on the way home, where he christened me the "Irish Chupacabra".

12 Him Playing with my kid....and my cats.

...and that's not to mention the incident in Clontarf Castle where Tony in his broadest English accent told the girl...Don't worry chick.. I'm Irish!

and more importantly...

13: Him ringing me from the UK offering me his support when politics and my own shenanigans saw me leave my Sensei.

14 Him offering me the full repertoire of instructors he has at his disposal to help me.

Tony has his detractors. He doesn't do "NORMAL" Martial Arts. He does Tony's Martial Art's, He is someone I should spend more time with, but don't. He is someone I don't contact enough, but did today.

What I will say is, that WHEN Tony drives the golf-ball out of his chest, and recovers (depending on next weeks full body scan) and is ready....YOU WILL ALL BE PILLAGED.

Best wishes T........from everyone in our dojo.

Tony Bailey
Can all my friends who are in training please set aside some time for something important after class
Thanks so much xx

Tony had arranged a load of friends to do some Reiki remote healing. I felt their energy and love. Wonderful, wonderful, wonderful.

Tony Bailey
"Apologies to Loki Photography for my addition, but it suits the message. Mr P, you have an army of support with you bigger than any other, batten down the hatches Cancer, there's HUGE fight about to go off !!! "

Someone talked to me last night about how they cannot understand my putting up a blow by blow account of what is going on with my illness. I will tell you this.... I have had many pm's from people who are suffering either themselves or members of their family who have said my attitude to the disease is helping them...so that's a good thing ....Too fucking right? , They said I like being the centre of attention !! Too fucking right. But it is my energy vampire self which is drawing MASSIVE amounts of great positiveness from all my many friends and acquaintances around the world. I PROMISE YOU that if it wasn't for all the messages and interactions I would not be in a great place right now ..... so thank you all very much
I have lived much of my life on FB over the years. I have been told I annoy, I inspire, I help, I piss off...so all just like real life then. I'm not stopping doing that in any way, shape or form .

I bloody love my life and the people who are in it. I even love my tumour ...that's right you didn't misread this. I will love it until I have it cut out in a week or so. It's a part of me currently. But believe you me I will get through this with your love and support. I am terribly thin now.... I call it cancer chic as my diet is now just raw or gently cooked veggies... NO FUCKING CAKE damn, damn, damn. I am juicing, taking Vitamin B17 until I feel sick, Colon cleanse every day, every conceivable vitamin and dietary aid .... but I am strong and will get through I promise you lot....why ? cos I bloody well will !!

What I neglected to tell people on this post was that for the previous two weeks I had spent an hour on the floor of my bathroom every morning giving myself coffee enema's as apparently they help purge the bile ducts of your liver. This boosts the immune system. I cannot even begin to tell you what a horrible and demeaning thing this is. To cap it all I'm doing it to myself. It made me realize though just how much I wanted to live. I have spoken to many cancer sufferers who after being told what this particular protocol was about and was for, they just turned their noses up and said they would never do this in a million years. Frankly then, the gift of life weighs little on your shoulders. This is a battle and it has to be won and I was prepared to do whatever it takes to fucking win, even pooing all over my bathroom floor when my timing wasn't great. Had to be done though.

November 14 2014
Been to the docs this morning (The family GP of many years standing.) He reckons if the operation is a success ...six months out. Also they will have to hacksaw my chest open to get to it .... much akin to open heart surgery. Operation is a major one.

Bollocks and there was me thinking a local anesthetic with a cup of tea and possible cake.

I'm very much looking forward to this weekend
It may well be my last before the operation
Dojo in the morning
Rugby with Richard Barnes
MAI awards with so many friends on Sunday
Bloody brilliant
Thank you all again for all the private messages today
Truly humbled
Namaste xx

Please share
Next Monday may be the last time I teach for a few months. Please everyone come along to the 7.00 pm class and lets go out in some style. I'd welcome all my old students back for a night on the mats...thank you

Little did I know that this post was to give me one of the best evenings of my life.

November 14 2014

From my friend Stuart Welch very humbling I haven't sent much vocal support your way recently Tony which I apologise for, but I think it's because before tonight it hadn't really hit me what is actually happening to you, like if I ignored it, it wouldn't be true. Tonight I heard you tell us you're frightened, and that scared me because you are the hardest bastard I know! I won't say goodbye though because you are going to beat this. You are going to beat this because you are Anthony Pillage and you are hard as fucking nails! I have tried before to imagine my life, and the club, without you but I can't. I don't think of you as a human, with the possibility of not being here tomorrow. I think of you as Tony; the force that will just keep going and going. You are the only person to have introduced me to proper martial arts. You opened my eyes to a vast culture, which spreads further and deeper than I could have imagined. You awarded me my black belt- probably my proudest achievement- when 10 years ago I thought martial arts was all about ancient teachings which were only passed on to the elite. But I am here today, a happier, and more enlightened, humbled and stronger character because of you, your teachings and the extension of your friendship- something which I never thought I would appreciate as much as I do. We will all see you on the other side, after they remove that lump and you begin the road to recovery. You will do this because I believe in you as you have believed in me and everyone else at WOTSW over the years. We all love you Tony and we can't wait to see you back in training mate and inflicting some more pain. Namaste brother:')

November 16 2014
Don't forget it's my last class teaching this Monday at seven. I invite all my old students back for a one off special class ...... will be epic. (*it was*)

November 17 2014
What an amazing evening last night at the MAI awards. I genuinely could not believe the outpouring of love, support and genuine affection as well as the amount of people who wished me well. Great night and thank you all
I received a Life Time Achievement award...Great to catch up with soon many fabulous friends

As this story unfolds this awards ceremony was to be the life changer I never dreamed of.

The defining picture of the journey was taken that night. I looked like Paul Gascoigne's crystal meth addicted, seventy-eight year old brother. I think I was down to 13 stone and was standing next to the magnificently hunky Ian 'The Machine' Freeman. I looked so ill. I often though looked at that pic to remind me just how far I had come over the following 12 months.

When presented with his award, my friend Kevin Mills stood up and asked who would be interested in doing a charity seminar to help me and the dojo. I believe that something like sixty of the country's top instructors put their name down to help that night alone. Jenni, Kevin's wife, came up with the name Warriors Assemble *and the charity was born in a heartbeat. I would guess*

thirty people getting their Hall of Fame induction spoke in kind words about The Pillage and dedicated their award to me. Wow just wow...feeling loved is a beautiful thing even if it comes from a hairy twenty stone cage fighter. I left there that evening so damn happy and nourished beyond belief. An evening of unforgettable magnitude.

I remember getting The Lifetime Achievement Award. I got on stage and was presented with the certificate and said "I'm only getting this because you think I'll be dead by the time the next one comes around".

After talking to friends subsequently many actually thought after seeing me that this would indeed be true. The other recipients of the highest accolade that night were Maurice 'Mo' Teague and Ian 'The Machine' Freeman. I wasn't worthy to be on the same stage as these giants but it did feel mightily good.

Losing weight, keeping sane (just)

The Classes

My favourite song is from the band Elbow One Day Like This. *I have seen it sung live on, I believe, seven occasions and once at Glastonbury where I sang the words with over 100,000 enraptured souls on a magical evening in front of the Pyramid stage.*

In my mind I'm sure we all have had that day, that amazing occasion which has nourished us for an eternity. I had two of these during this small period of time. The dates aren't important.

On a good night I may get thirty people on the mats for the Monday self-defence class.

I put up this post on Facebook
"Next Monday may be the last time I teach for a few months. Please everyone come along to the 7.00 pm class and lets go out in some style. I'd welcome all my old students back for a night on the mats...thank you"
I knew in my mind there was far more to this post than originally met the eye. I had the nagging doubt that maybe this would be the last class I ever taught. The operation was looming and I obviously had absolutely no idea as to what I would be capable of afterwards or even if I was going to survive the surgery. Maybe I would die during the operation (a 12% chance) or not regain enough functionality to teach properly ever again.

At 6.30 pm the first unusual face turned up. My old mate Steve Strong had driven up from Dagenham. Whilst greeting him, the mighty Walloper, Gavin Richardson lurched from the car park. Friend after friend, old students (including one who had got a train down from York for the class and travelled home the same evening) training partners and instructors congregated from all over the UK. Seventy-six students had taken the time to come and support me on what could have been a final HUZZAH.

On three occasions I had to leave the mat as my eyes betrayed the deep emotions I was feeling. I have seldom been more touched or felt genuine love and affection like I did over the following two hours. I soaked up every bit of energy these beautiful people gave me and revelled in it. I taught a brilliant class and left to rapturous applause. One day a year like this will see me right. Too fucking true.

The second one was I had the idea of doing a seminar with two of my closest friends. The far too handsome Mikey Wright and Guru Eddie Quinn. Not only two consummate martial artists but also two consummate human beings. We decided that we would call it The Approach (Eddie's baby), The System (Mikey's Defence Lab and Systema) and the Poison (my pressure points). It worked like a dream with again over 70 people taking part. It turned out to be the best seminar I have ever attended let alone taught on. The energy in the room was buzzing, the humour was flowing and I was in one of my 'don't give a fuck if I show off' moods. The students lapped it up and again we left to tumultuous applause. Apart from Tony Bailey there would have been no finer people I could ever of have been more proud to share a mat with. I was honored beyond belief.

One day a year like this will see me right...fuck that, I'd had two.

November 19 2014
Today is my scary day
PET scan and a load of nuclear medicine
The results from this could well define the rest of my life
Wish me luck mon amies
Bit tired, very little sleep
I'm out now more nuclear charged than a prawn bathing near
Fukashima or a goat near Chernobyl
Can wait to see if my willy glows in the dark tonight
One step closer to getting better
Love you all xx
Namaste

For those of you who are unfamiliar with this procedure let me elucidate. They inject you with radioactive glucose. The cancer thinks mmmmm numnum time and gobbles it. It then shows up if the little bastard has started to go walkabout.

I AM THE TUMOURNATOR !!!!!!!

I just had this on my wall. I haven't stopped laughing yet...quite brilliant. Richard Jones thank you mate
"All the very best Anthony Pillage ... I met you once, you made a strange buzzing noise as you nipple gripped me and I unceremoniously fell down like a sack of shit... But you made a lasting impression and I find your recent posts about your latest adversary truly inspiring! Go kick the "C" in the nuts mate! "
The Pillage Army as people were calling themselves was growing day by day and it felt marvelous beyond belief.

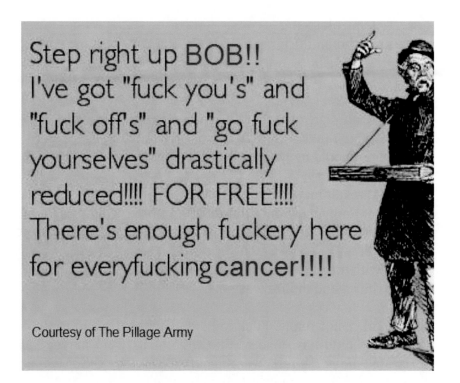

Step right up BOB!!
I've got "fuck you's" and
"fuck off's" and "go fuck
yourselves" drastically
reduced!!!! FOR FREE!!!!
There's enough fuckery here
for everyfucking cancer!!!!

Courtesy of The Pillage Army

From Adrian Starr-Sensei wise words:

"Death implies life.
Some people are lucky enough to get to prepare for death and
say goodbye properly.
Some are taken with no warning - leaving so many words unsaid
that should have been said.
Live every day as though you have been told it's your last; leave
no love unloved, no kind words unsaid and no life unlived.
Live, love, be loved, die and move on."
November 21 2014
Just had a call from the hospital
Meeting today at 12.25pm aghhhh its poopy time

Forget all my bluster
More scared than the gimp in Pulp Fiction !!

Later that day.

However, no sign of secondary tumours from the PET scan
which is a big relief
The tumour could be lymphoma or thymus based
Biopsy on Tuesday
Not a bad result maybe
It appears I only have one tumour...therefore I will be calling it
BOB !! Why you ask....it is simple. Every time BOB appears it
gets fucked by FLASHHEART !!!!
Who is with me with a resounding WOOF !!!!!!!!!
And so the legend of Bob was born

Not a bad result really. Fuck me sideways that was the BEST
news one could have had at that time apart from maybe *"oh
sorry Mr Pillage the tests were negative it was a spec of jam on
the optics"* or some other bloody nonsense !

November 22 2014
Nice relaxing day spent with good friends and rugby !!
However BOB the tumour seems a little agitated tonight. Really
bad chest pains ..... little wanker ......

November 23 2014
I wonder if I went BUPA I could bribe the surgeon to make the
chest incision to look like a huge shark bite !! Thanks Eddie
Quinn for the idea this morning mate..... (I actually asked Mr
Marzouk if this was indeed possible, he just looked at me. I
think the word would be pityingly!!)

I've had a quiet day today as Bob the magic tumor has been playing up ...
The little tinker
Hope they get a date soon for his removal
I have a lava lamp and some paperweights to produce as Xmas gifts

This was not actually the joke that it seems. My mate Anton, an odd and wonderful chap had worked out a way to plasticise the tumour and put it into a lava lamp as a memento. Sadly Mr. Marzouk, my surgeon, wouldn't let me keep it otherwise I promise that this would have happened.

November 24 2014
Matthew Sylvester to Tony
"Just saw the news, best wishes Tony, I'm sure your going to give this bastard a battle worthy of legends!"

Just starting to get a little nervous about my biopsy tomorrow
Apparently being drilled through my sternum whilst awake
Hopefully without popping a lung

November 25 2014
Not sure if there is a bloody bed for me now
Oh bollocks
Then we got a call saying come over immediately we can do the biopsy right now. Can you imagine living on tenterhooks knowing that in a few hours someone is going to be drilling a hole in your sternum whilst you are awake. Then they cant, then they can. Fuck me my resolve is dwindling with every passing minute.
Fuck fuck fuck
Get here, no pissing bed

Really angry
Looks like another week of waiting

In hindsight this was the equivalent of me winning the lottery. Had this procedure taken place Bob (who was pretty much self-contained) would have popped if they had gone ahead, sending cancer cells throughout my body. This was one of seven incidents that potentially could have been bad, and I mean REALLY bad, but didn't happen. I am not a huge believer in God but I am sure someone or something was looking after me at this time. I thank this 'person' on a pretty regular basis even today...actually especially now.

Right from day one the advice from one and all had been to go along the NHS route as they have a better support team in place. After this latest cock up, my Macmillan nurse said you need to get this under way now Mr. Pillage. My advice is to go the BUPA route and do it quickly. Bless her she made an appointment there and then with one of the top Thoracic surgeons in the world, a Mr. Joseph Marzouk. I had no idea that the University College Hospital in Coventry boasted a pioneering and renowned Cardiac Thoracic unit. Were the Gods conspiring yet again to keep me safe? I think so.

It was also funny that at this time I became a little more stoic and belligerent. The cancer card mentality if you like. You fuck off I've got cancer, I want to sit there...I've got cancer, I want the last piece of cake...I've got cancer. You get the drift I guess. You also find weirdly that cancer is like the most potent pheromone spray. It makes you interesting and the centre of attention and I have never felt so popular.

November 26 2014

After all the tooing and froing yesterday with the hospital, I admit I wasn't in a great place last night.......really sank home. However, this morning me and BOB have reached a good level of understanding. If he stops pressing into my lung for a few hours I will not play Justin Bieber records at him for a day....an amicable truce I think

Are there any kind souls about on Friday who could give me a lift to the Walsgrave Hospital at 11.15am

I can never get the mighty Hummer parked up there

Thanks

November 27 2014

Well tomorrow is looming quickly and I believe the meeting I will have tomorrow will be the defining one. I've gone Private to see Mr Marzouk . I hope I will now get some bloody answers as thus far I have not really.

HUGE thanks to all the hundreds of good wishes and messages coming through ... brilliant. Also to Sarah Pillage who has helped me keep what little is left of my sanity.

Sarah has always told me that BUPA was a brilliant investment. This could not have happened without their full and complete support. I urge you to sign up they were amazing with me.

November 28 2014

On my way to hospital

Anxious moi? cest possible !

I've just read that Katie fucking Price has called one of her new breast implants Bob

Bob is not happy

There can be only one !!!!! He is the Connor McLoud of tumours

I'm being admitted Sunday evening for my operation first thing on Monday morning

Prognosis seems better than I could have reasonably hoped for as it is operable

Bob you is fucked matey

Lovely surgeon

Apparently they seal my sternum up with wire

I am Ironman

Let's dooooooooooo it !

Its certainly been a roller coaster few weeks ....from the initial diagnosis of being told a tumour growing from your pericardium (little chance of survival) to today "we think it is self contained" and can treat it.... to the GREAT fortune of not having the biopsy on Wednesday which may well have spread it should it be lymphoma.

I would just like to say this.......I could not have endured the trials and tribulations without the massive love and support of all you guys on here and the constant daily phone calls and messages from friends like John Hammill, Ian Goehler, Steve Strong, Kwoklyn Wan, Anton Beasley, Nathan Hendry, Andy Gibney, Chetna'Mahesh Kothavale, Eddie Quinn, Mikey Wright and so many others. You have kept me strong as has the ever wondrous Sarah Pillage who has been truly incredible.

My warmest thanks also go to Mike Knight, Andy Haynes, Martin Hughes, Richard Green and Devon Dunk for keeping the dojo alive and vibrant.

One special mention has to go to Richard Barnes and his lovely family for putting up with me every Saturday for the RUGBY internationals.

I hope to be back teaching by the February weekend of Awesomeness arranged by Kevin Mills bless him.

I will be out of circulation I am guessing till Wednesday. After that I expect many visitors bringing gifts of wonder to my bedside !!!!
Thank you all again so very, very much

Let me fill you in a little of my meeting with Mr. Marzouk. The minute I was ushered into his office I could tell I was in the presence of greatness. He explained in great detail the operation and how they would do the biopsy when he was in there rummaging around. I was my normal foolish, nay, puckish self. I did ask him whether he could do the scar like a shark bite. He politely laughed as he did when he asked me what time on the MONDAY (yes the following Monday, only 3 days away) I would like. Shit just got real so I asked him "when do you do your best work?" "Morning," he said and I was booked in. He did one more operation after me before he went off on long term sick leave. Again were the Gods' conspiring?

November 29 2014

I was asked yesterday had I done any deals with god over the cancer and the operation. An interesting question as I remember doing them when my Grandad was ill and dying of cancer when I was a teenager. You see this horrible disease has wiped out Grandad, Mum, Auntie, Uncle all on my Mum's side. I have always been terrified of it but when diagnosed I was a lot different to how I thought I would feel.
People keep saying I have inspired them over my handling of this...let me tell you very few people have been privy to the tears I have shed on many occasions during this whole process. Strangely it's been when people have been nice to me rather than when bad news has come and battered me. So have I done a deal with God?...the answer is no. But I have done a deal with myself as God of my own universe FACT. I will fight this all the

way..... fact. I will recover far faster than is humanly possible, I will use my voice to far better affect to help people and learn more of the healing arts. I will spend more time with friends, I will do the things I have procrastinated over for bloody years, I will be the very best incarnation of me that I possibly can. I will remember how very blessed I am. So I am in for a many months of pain....so be it. I realise how lucky I am. Lets get this over and done with and start to heal. I'm bored of being inactive.

So if there is a god I say thank you for this its has made me realise many things.

Now let me get better quickly as I have a shit load of stuff to do !!

Also I have a ticket for Glasto next year...I owe my dear friends Sarah Clarke and Daryl Clarke a night in Shangri-La hahahaha I also promised the Millses that I would teach on their summer camp.

I made both...just.

November 30 2014

In at Hospital today at 7pm. Gonna enjoy a beautiful day with my pal Tony Bailey

Thought Fargo Village in the sun may be nice.

Oh bugger

Hospital called wanted come in earlier than expected

I will try and write a bit later

If not all being well I'll be back on line Thursday

It's been emotional xx

Btw great day with Tony Bailey

Always a pleasure and surprisingly solved the Jack the Ripper murders

There are times in your life which become defining moments

Tomorrow is certainly one for me

I am sitting in my hospital bed scared beyond belief and lonely

Over the past weeks with all the support and love I have received one person stands out beyond all measure and that is Sarah Pillage

I honestly can't thank you enough Hutchy

Please everyone give her the support she will need until I get better

She is one in a million

I am blessed to know you

A woman of substance

Bless you xxxx

Let's get this day into a perspective. I first met Tony Bailey on a training camp in Cyprus where he was teaching. I was immediately struck by his gentle demeanor and rather beautiful energy. Over the following ten years we became firm friends. He is also my Reiki instructor. He is also one of the most dangerous men I know. We now do seminars together as General Pain or The Twin Towers of Tony. It is a huge honour to have this man as my friend.

When he heard of my operation date he came up to visit and spent the day talking and putting perspectives back into my life. He also gave me a t-shirt with three Grim Reapers in a waiting room with the phrase, "I know, they never told me it was Pillage either! Might as well go home." I laughed and wore it into hospital later. No-one on this planet could have done more for me that day. We walked around Stratford upon Avon, had a wonderful Thai meal overlooking the river then made our way back to Coventry. No words of mine could ever do justice as to what that man did for me. I will always be totally indebted to you, sir, for that kindness. Sadly the phone went and the hospital wanted me in two hours earlier than I had planned. That's it I'm in ....no turning back time. Scared? You have no idea.

However, fate was with me yet again. When I arrived at the ward I was greeted by the mum of two of my students, the lovely Chetna Kotavale. Blimey did that help or what? She made sure I was looked after and then some. At about 10 pm I wandered outside to get a breath of fresh air and I admit I had a smoke. I hadn't had one for over two months and the heady fumes of a tasty cigar made me feel woozy. Fuck it! Then had another, it may have been the last. It tasted vile though.

Cutting Bob

December 1 2014
As you can imagine I didn't get a lot of sleep last night
I've made my peace with the world I hope
I am starting the road to getting better today
Loads of pain as haven't had my painkillers
Bob needs to fuck off now
See you all soon xx
One hour until operation
Starting to think it might be a good idea to open Charlie tunnel
and escape via my cunning wooden horse contraption
They are getting suspicious with all the earth falling out of my
theatre gown hem
I'm off
Tata
Get your hands off my penis!!

Let's elaborate a tad. The chap in the bed opposite was a chatty soul going in for a bypass operation. He had been there for two weeks awaiting his procedure and had seen loads of people going down for their operations: "Don't worry." he said jovially "they'll give you some happy pills about half an hour before they take you down, you'll be fine." I waited and waited and watched his pills take hold ten minutes after they administered them. Mr. Happy wasn't even in it as he was giggling and waving on the way to his operation. I thought, 'Brilliant that'll be me shortly.' Then at 8.07am they turned up to wheel me to theatre: "No happy pills?" I asked. "No, your anesthetist doesn't agree with them." SHITTY MCSHIITYBOSATFACE! I'm screwed. They wheeled me to the ante-room. "MMMMm maybe this is a mistake, I have no cancer I can make a run for it." I thought in a maniacal and frightened thought bubble. Mr. Marzouk then walked in gowned up. Fuck it! I thought with my bravado meter running at the same score as a Norwegian Eurovision entrants score of nil point!! A few seconds later I had the injection that was to send me to sleep for the next seven hours.

I also loved the fact that were I to die on the operating table my last words on the earth would be the quote by Charles Souza: "Get your hands off my penis." If you haven't seen it type in the phrase on YouTube and watch it twice, it's the best thing ever. That's the way to leave them hanging and what a bloody epitaph. It still makes me chuckle, even today.

Sarah Pillage update

Rightio Anthony Pillage update: (bit like Badger Watch but less badgery)

Surgery went OK. He's very sleepy and in lots of pain (typical man, you'd think he'd had a major operation or summat). Couldn't get it all out as it was attached to major blood vessels, so they've left a teeny bit and he'll have to have radiotherapy on it as soon as he's healed enough. But otherwise, all's good. PS He wanted me to take a pic of him and post it. I took it but I won't.

PPS send me some money and I might. Send me even more, and I won't

PPPS A huge thanks for all the lovely messages. They really help x

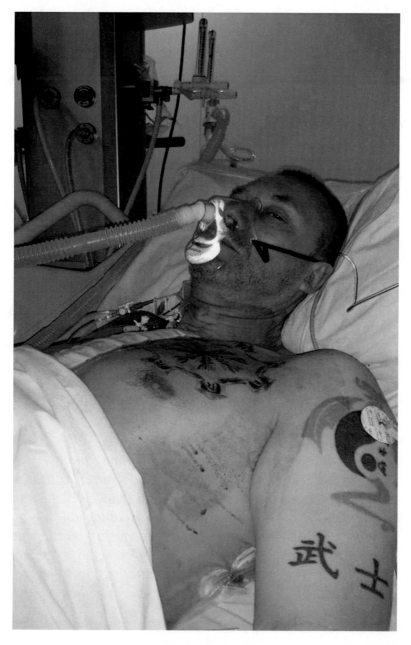

December 2 2014
I am out a day out early from high dependency unit.
Fucking broken.
They only managed to get 90% of Bob
But had to cut the phrenic nerve to my diaphragm to get to
some cancer that had wrapped around it. My right lung is now
bereft......
Basically got to learn to breathe again in a different way
So chemo here I come or radiotherapy but not for a while
Managed to walk about 30ft hence they have let me out
intensive care.
A lot of morphine
But baby I am alive and grateful beyond measure xx
And I'm out early even though they had to collapse a lung to
get to some other bits
I'm shattered and sore but can't tell you how good it feels to be
alive
A man who I was chatting to Sunday night with not a dissimilar
op died this morning
I have been lucky
I remember also singing the Wizard of Oz song Ding Dong the
Bob is dead. Weird Moi? Most fucking certainly.

*I think this is my favorite tale from this time. In my bay there
were four patients each with a nurse with them 24/7. The two in
the beds opposite were pretty comatose. However, the man on
my left was a complete cockwomble. Moaning all day at the
nursing staff (who were absolutely wonderful), cutting across
them and generally being despicable and rude. My mate Richard
Barnes turned up to chat. Rich is one of my fave people and
squash partner. I loved sitting putting the world to rights after
me trouncing him on the courts.*

Captain Cock head then tried to engage him in conversation. I lost it BIG TIME.

Now let's get a perspective. The day before I had been literally cut in half. I had two drains in my stomach the size of small swords. The cannula in my neck's spike was so long they had to have a crash team on standby when inserting it. I think I had nine drugs going through it. My chest was held together by wire. I had a catheter and two cannulas in my hands. I removed the oxygen mask and somehow pulled myself forward enough to see past the intervening curtain. I saw the chap, an Asian man in his 40's I would guess. Richard had absolutely no idea what the hell was going on and looked at me quizzically.

In some strange and somewhat posh voice I rasped: "You there, shut up he's my visitor. If you speak to him again I'll kill you. Now fuck orf." With that last expletive I apparently collapsed. Rich spoke to me some time later about it. He said: "I stopped worrying about you then, I knew you were back to your belligerent best."

Sarah also reminded me that this was also the time when I found I could breathe out the oxygen in a fine smoky mist. Apparently saying: "Look Hutchy, I'm a Dragon." Whilst also humming the notes from the machine registering my vital statistics. Morphine, a wonderful bedfellow in such times. I salute thee with awesomeness fella!!

You see having the myriad of visitors over the ensuing weeks helped enormously but in truth even surrounded by your closest friends and favourite people it does feel incredibly lonely because no one can understand what you are going through either in you

59

bemused head or in your broken body. No-one, and that is an awful torturous thing.

People will say to you such platitudes as "be strong," "hang in there," "you can do it." However my all-time fave is of course the ubiquitous "You're a fighter …you'll beat it." I know people mean well, but it's bollocks isn't it? Maybe the stigma of cancer just makes people talk shite. The fact is we are strong, we are not going to give up but frankly your platitudes and inanity are, at best, meaningless. The fact is you have cancer, end of, and you will deal with it in your own way.

I, of course, am a fricking hypocrite. The year before, my friend Lee Conchie Davis had died of complications arising from his treatment of leukemia. I had found out that he went to the doctors with a headache but further tests had showed he had a brain aneurism and only had days to live. I apprehensively picked up the phone and he answered immediately. What I said next will haunt me for eternity: "How are you mate?" As soon as I said it I cringed. Lee however was always a gentleman and brushed off my faux pas, thank god, with his normal good grace and humour. He died four days later surrounded by his family. I asked him though was there anything I could do for him: "Yes" he answered, "You big, gobby bastard, go and make people aware of how they can help people like me, with leukemia, by donating bone marrow." We contacted the Blood Cancer Group and thus far have got over 200 people on the register. I know of at least two matches from these people, so some good has already come from this tragic experience.

December 3 2014
I feel rough today
I mean really rough.

At least they have agreed the cannula can come out of my neck
I'm at the BMI Hospital Meriden at Wallsgrave now. Long
visiting hours
All welcome
My new target is to get out by the weekend

December 4 2014
Easily the most uncomfortable night ever faced by anyone in
the history of the world ever
At one point I couldn't move and couldn't reach the nurse bell
Oh and couldn't breath. I honestly thought I was going to die.

*Again let me elaborate. As this was the night I nearly passed on
big style. Over the past few days I had had little sleep, if any.
When they put me in a private room I was glad of the peace and
quiet. However, when I crashed out I must have tried to
maneuver myself to get comfortable whilst asleep. The upshot
was that somehow I had bowed myself over the bed. I couldn't
breathe at all and was in agony. I couldn't reach the nurse alarm
or my phone. Luckily I managed to hook my foot in the bed head
and pulled myself back up. Pillage's nine lives at least one down.
Fuck, did it hurt? Loads.*

Even after three days my blood stats won't go above 93%.
Sadly another day on an oxygen mask. I feel like the path of my
life is strewn with cowpats from the Devil's own satanic herd.
Ok just spoken with Doctor Parmar (Mr Marzouk's
replacement as he was now off ill himself) re the operation for
the first time personally.
Seems the operation was very very very fucking nasty.
The right lung is now not working as the diaphragm nerve
(phrenic) is severed so will need an operation to restore at

some point. The lung was collapsed to remove some cancer behind it and has caused lack of drainage so another reason why I'm not breathing well

There has been long term drain into the heart from the tumour so that may have longer term issues.

It didn't help it was bigger than a grapefruit .

I may be allowed home at the weekend .

So I feel lucky to be alive and will be enjoying it with a rather large toodle pip !!

This was the first time a fruit analogy was made about Bob. Wilko's was the size of a pineapple when he had his. I feel cheated!

December 5 2014

Huzzah I've actually had 5 hours sleep
Feel reasonably good
Hopeful of getting out of here tomorrow
I need to do a poo big time
But struggling
All I hear all morning is the bloody song from Frozen
"Let it Go" seriously 5 times on radio or bloody TV.
Is the universe that unsubtle really !!!
All joking aside the two hour strain of

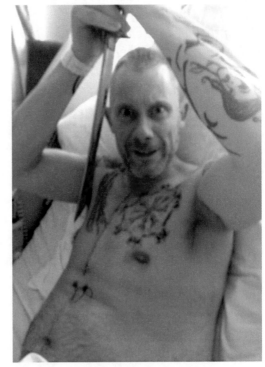

trying to have a shit this morning has left me absolutely
broken - beyond all measure
Hope I feel better in the morning
Cos right now I couldn't even fight an aubergine or Guy Bloom
In lots of agony
Just spoke to the nurse re the new pain
"Feels like broken ribs" I say
"It probably is where they cracked you open" says she
"You're only feeling it now as the anesthesia has worn off"
Fuck me no wonder I'm delicate
Still bloody gorgeous and ruggedly handsome though xx
Just wanted to say what a truly wonderful you bunch are
My world has shrunk to that of a room
All your good wishes messages funnies rants are 100000%
helping me keep going
Namaste my friends xxx

December 6 2014
I've been let out today
Can't believe it
Off home for a cup of tea and a doughnut
I think you guys have made a difference of a couple of days at
least to getting me out of this hospital
Whoop and a WOOF
The badger has gone feral again !!!
Seriously can everyone take a note of this
I never realised exactly how ill I was and probably still am
However what has made me in a position where this weekend
I am allowed out and moreover alive has been the hugely
professional and caring nature of the medical and nursing staff
at the Wallsgrave and BMI hospitals
They have been wonderful and I thank each and every one of
them from the bottom of my heart

If you know a nurse please give them a hug from Mr P
Appreciate what they do a little more.

December 7 2014
Slept very well last night after a bit of a panicky start. I now have a bubble until Thursday when the histology results of the tumour come back....bit scared if I am honest. However, the sun is shining and I have five days to get a bit stronger and more petulent.
One of the great treasures of this year has been the friendship of Richard Barnes
Whose lovely daughters Hollie Barnes and Lucie
Barnes delivered the finest Xmas selection basket to keep a Pillage amused
Driven ably by Sue Barnes (like)
Thank you so much chaps
The card alone has given me hours of fun xxx

Let me define what I mean by the term 'bubble'. Since day one the time between appointments or results I placed myself in a mental protective bubble. There was nothing I could do to change what was happening so I decided to just ignore anything going on until I needed to. It worked. Oh God! Did it work. It certainly saved my sanity at times.

December 8 2014
One week ago I was being operated on
What a bloody week that's been
Phew

December 9 2014
Goal today is to walk to the end of my road

Will I do it
Of course I bloody well will X
Oh shit
Had an un-braced cough
I may have pulled a stomach muscle and opened a rib up again
That bloody hurt
Struggling with my breathing today but I have to realize, I only have one lung and broken ribs plus a split sternum. Still a bit panicky though x

Truth is I did about twenty yards and had to come home. The cough was agony. They teach you to cough by holding a pillow to your chest. This one just hit me like a missile from Beelzebub's rocket silo so had no chance to grab anything. I thought I was going to split in half. It later transpired that I had five broken ribs on the left hand side and three on the right. Eighteen months later I am still having problems with two of them. No wonder it hurt.

December 10 2014
Feel really depressed and low tonight
Lots of pain and hate the bed soaking night sweats that I know are coming
If anyone has any spare energy send some my way please *mon amie's*

December 11 2014
Last night I was really down in the dumps. (Certainly the worst since the operation) You lot responded magnificently and VOILA I am feeling perky today. It just goes to show once again the collective power of good people doing good things for the right reasons. When I am better I am formulating something where we can help people going through illness but are

alone......we all need, I believe, to reach out and help those people who have no one. I can't think of anything worse... However HUGE thanks again to all of you seriously xxxxxxx
My new target I have set myself is teaching by mid-February I think that is achievable and honest

December 12 2014
I realised something last night....we once had a t-shirt slogan at the club "More Hugs than Thugs"
Because of my operation and the paranoia of catching any germs I haven't hugged anyone for a couple of weeks
This sucks. It's amazing how the touch and feel of another heartbeat can make so much difference to someone. Imagine you are someone who hasn't had that interaction for years...
Go on I dare ya...give someone a hug and make their day today
I miss hugs

December 13 2014
Someone says it's the little battles that will mean the most.
TWO days now no night sweats...SO happy
Scar looking good
Eleven days ago I was cut in half
Wish they had done it in the shape of a shark bite
And sort of managed to have a bloody bath
The Badgers Nadgers of watery splashy fun

December 14 2014
I feel the need to share some thoughts this afternoon. I am planning to pop in to our Xmas grading just for 5 minutes to see everyone and say hi from a distance. I will be wearing a facemask to stop me getting any germs and carrying a walking stick to ward people away if necessary. All my adult life I have

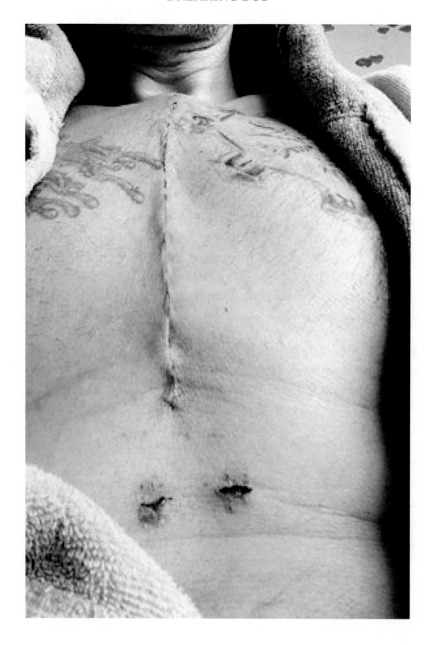

been a big rambunctious sort of bloke ...more than capable of looking after myself.

Today I feel genuinely scared because I am vulnerable. I forgot what this emotion was and is. I really don't like it at all. I do know that I will be far more mindful of the elderly, weaker or disabled now when I go out and about when I am better.

I've been back home now

Glad I went

Well done everyone

Thanks again to Stephanie Woodward, Mike Knight and Devon Dunk. Andy Haynes for being so fabulous xxx

It was brilliant btw. The journey though was a nightmare. It took me 20 mins to negotiate my front door step. Every bump in the car was piercing. But the welcome I got was worth it beyond measure from both students and parents alike. I felt blessed and took myself home with another small victory won.

December 16 2014

My buddy Carl Shell sent me a lovely parcel of goodies that arrived today to keep me entertained and all that malarky. Thank you sir much appreciated !!

My chest feels a little better today again but the broken ribs are still playing up. Actually went out today for ten mins WHOOOOOOP.

Still awaiting the results of the cancer biopsy to see the path to take....very nervous as I am sure you can imagine. Bob is nearly gone...the little tinker. (*He wasn't*)

Ahhhh poor Sarah has come back from the club with severe sickness

I really hope and pray it isn't contagious cos if it is I'm in trouble

Feeling helpless

December 19 2014
Well the good news is that this week I have added about 20% on my lung capacity spirometer dewberry thing, which is great, plus I actually managed to have a proper bath. Baby steps I know but all in the right direction thank Jupiter and his mighty cock !!

December 21 2014
Not a great day today health wise
Finding it a bit troublesome breathing
This one lung collapsed malarky is starting to wear a little thin
Still got a big day planned with my loverrrrrrrr Richard
Olpin coming up for the day
They said there would be good and bad days
This was a crap one

December 23 2014
Just finished major chat with Doctors
Seems I'm mostly healing well apart from a potential hernia (it wasn't)
Marvelous !!
I think I've overdone it over the past two days
In bloody agony
Time to rest and recoup some

It was now some three weeks after the operation. The process thus far had been scary beyond belief, shocking, painful and life threatening. But there is a sort of ceremony about the whole thing starting from the moment you get your initial diagnosis. Not only from the medical professionals involved but from friends and family. Actually, no, that's absolute bollocks I had NO support from ANY of my family, probably as I didn't want them to know. But friends do the good stuff. They send cards, bring presents, send DVD's and books to keep you sane and engaged. You get an amazing stream of visitors until they think that you are going to survive, then they fuck off and it's actually quite lonely. You almost get addicted to the attention, which is weird. Actually that's probably just me if I'm honest.

December 24 2014

Got to go back to the hospital today, been awake hours with my chest and arms in spasm. Have to admit to more than a few tears last night the pain was so bad. At one point in bed I actually couldn't move. I don't know if its the walking or maneuvering in the bath that has caused this but back to week one pain levels again....... BOLLOCKY BAH HUMBUG !!

They've put me on morphine again, as well as Diclophenic, Paracetamol and Codeine

Shit I could pierce my nipples with a katana and not feel a thing.

Some bad news

I ran into the consultant dealing with my case and managed a ten minute chat

There is nothing they can do about my collapsed lung apart from pin the diaphragm back with another operation. That would give me a little more oxygen circulation but not a huge amount.

Looks like I'll only be working on half capacity from now on

Radiotherapy and / or Chemo looming in the New Year

Not the best news eh

Well may I take this opportunity to wish all my friends and students a wonderful holiday and a fantastic Xmas.

Even with morphine I'm still in absolute bloody agony tonight

Just want to sleep and wake up feeling a little better

This is bloody horrible and I really don't know what has bought this on with such intensity.

December 25 2014

Many thanks for all the private message's and texts. I feel a bit less in pain today.... they said I would have bad days and good days. So after lunch Sarah is off to her Mums and I will be sitting down and watching for the first time A Wonderful Life with the magnificent James Stewart. Bloody Rock N Roll lifestyle me. Seriously to all my friends I hope you and your family have the very best of days today and the coming year holds only pleasant surprises xx

This post does not even vaguely get to the bottom (yes pun intended) of what happened to me on this strangely unforgettable Xmas day. One of my students Gary Breen had kindly dropped off a brilliant Chrimbo present, Thor's Hammer 'Moljnor'. I was so pleased, although I was so weak I couldn't even vaguely pick it up. It now sits on my desk as a reminder of that terrible day. It was quite ironic that I couldn't even lift it an inch through my weakness from everything. Only the Mighty Thor could apparently pick it up in the legends (and, of course, Marvel Films). I use this as a mental yardstick of just how far I have come. Cheers Breeny Baby for such a truly wonderful gift. It actually took two months before I could lift it properly.

Sarah had cooked a lovely meal but we had eaten early so she could go over to see her Mum. I thought I would watch James Stewarts' It's A Wonderful Life...(Oh the fucking irony), have a glass of wine and relax.

Now if you have had an operation you know that it is awfully hard to get over the constipation caused by our old mate

morphine. Literally Sarah had walked out the door for ten seconds and I needed to poo. I gingerly ascended the stairs as I was still worried about falling and took my place on the loo. The poo had got stuck. Satan's log jam had kicked in. Now remember I had little internal musculature to even have a halfhearted push. I felt as if Bubba and his minions were forcing a reverse gang bang on my anus for over three, fucking, long, terrible hours. I screamed and screamed and could only come up with the solution of manually evacuating myself. Sometime later Sarah came back: "Did you have a nice time?" She enthusiastically enquired. My scowl spoke volumes. It wasn't the Xmas of my childhood dreams that was for sure. Yule Log? I think not.

December 26 2014

I'm not coping awfully well today with my breathing
I know it's early days in reality but the good lung left is the one
I had a pulmonary embolism in some years ago so doesn't
work as well as it should anyway.
I feel very bleak and scared today.
Not at all positive about anything
Guys so many thanks for all the support
Just had a perspective chat with the redoubtable Richard
Barnes always a pleasure spending time with this unique and
erudite man.
The reality is I had a bad couple of days and a crap morning
I could well of have been dead
I forgot this
Thanks Rich for the change of perspective mate xxxxxxxxxxxxx

December 27th 2014

My problem I think is the fact my back and arms seem to go into a spasm. This is what is causing the extreme pain as well as the tightness of my breathing. Any ideas people? Is this a residue from the operation or stress or the nerves growing back. Any ideas greatly appreciated.

December 28 2014
PILLAGES CHALLENGE TO YOU !!!
YES YOU........
I have woken up out of a lot of the bad pain I have felt over the past week, which is a great thing. But it has given me some thinking time.
I have just walked up my stairs and nearly passed out, as I was that much out of breath.
As many of you have joked over the years I was a heavy smoker. And by god in my mind I thought Id enjoyed every last one of them.... stupid sayings like "quitting is for losers". If I didn't have at least ten cigs on me I would have to go and buy some, even if it was relatively late at night.
On the day I found that there was an anomaly in my chest I quit. Stable door and horse a little eh !! That was after forty years of having smoked...I guess in that time I have quit for a total of maybe three weeks. AND YES I KNOW there is nothing more fucking hypocritical or annoying than an ex junkie or smoker.
MY CHALLENGE. PLEASE will five of you out there please consider giving up RIGHT NOW. There is the highest likelihood that you will get a disease linked to smoking if you continue. It's not too late...come on have some balls and do it. PLEASE don't go through what I am just for a fag...you are better than that.
If you don't give up smoking I will visit you late at night dressed like this.

Guys I thank you for saying I'm brave I really am not. I believe that this cancer was a result of my smoking for years. I just don't want anyone else if it is vaguely within my grasp to have to go through this. I can't actually go to bed as I am spasming that badly and can barely contain the tears welling up inside me. Just one person takes note now and all this I have gone through is worth it in my book. We take breathing for granted….don't FFS it's the scariest thing I have ever been through

December 29 2014
Morning all. Well we are now up to five people promising to quit smoking and another 4 to stop vaping. Well done to you all...now lets have some more. Thank you all

December 31 2014
New Year's Eve is like every other night; there is no pause in the march of the universe, no breathless moment of silence among created things that the passage of another twelve months may be noted; and yet no man has quite the same thoughts this evening that come with the coming of darkness on other nights.
To all my students and friends, may the next year fulfill you as people and grant you everything you deserve.
Namaste xx
I look back to this time last year and could not have even vaguely predicted the mayhem that 2014 bought into my life. Some of it was self - made, some probably as a result of my actions, some just the way things are dealt to you.
I go into the New Year slowly mending from major surgery but glad to be alive. I am uncertain of my future, as they still cannot tell me as to what the cancer I have actually is…. this scares the shit out of me. I have experienced the very best of British

Health Care as well as some of its worst.

However, as I look back as I do at this time every year I do not focus on this strangely but instead on the overwhelming feeling I get from 2014 is the value and sanctity of friendship and the unconditional love that this engenders. I am still overwhelmed by the outpouring of support I have had over the past few months, I promise you I would be in a far worse state had it not been for this.

I won't mention too many people as the list would take me until 12pm tonight to   shown the true spirit of goodness and looked after me superbly and had it not been for her support I shudder to think where I would be right now. Thank you Hutchy from the bottom of my heart

What advice can I offer to anyone of any note......DONT SMOKE might be a good one and fourteen brave souls have promised me they are giving up. Well done.

More importantly though is this. Live in the moment and enjoy every last second of that experience. Don't procrastinate and have those experiences NOW as the reality is if you don't the chance is you never will.

May 2015 bring you all peace, happiness and whatever floats your boat.

I shall be here next year have no fear.....

Namaste Mo Fo's xx

New Year, Still Here

2nd Jan 2015
I'm feeling a little depressed
For the first time I've studied the operation site and can see
just how much musculature I have lost and how completely
deformed my sternum now is
My hopes of a Vogue cover seem a long way away now.
Guy's thanks for the messages...I'm actually not depressed just
a little shocked on how deformed I am from the fine figure of a
man I was only a few weeks ago. Just have to work a little
harder on the mats when I am able to restore the Pillage
loveliness to its pristine glory x

3rd Jan 2015
I'm taking a 24 hour gamble and cutting my pain killers down
in half

5th Jan 2015
So truthfully how many of you guys that promised to quit
smoking have really done so.....mmm I think not

6th Jan 2015
I'm going into the dojo for a couple of hours work
tonight.....can't wait
I managed to drive in today...bloody chuffed

7th Jan 2015
Well I'm into day 2 of cutting down my painkillers

All good and been in to do a few hours work
Feeling bloody positive to be honest
#pillageisback

11th Jan 2015
Last week I was on 27 pain killers a day plus morphine... Today I will have only 10...... way to go meeeeeeeeeeeeee. Very bloody breathless though HATE IT

13th Jan 2015
I'm a little worried as my scar is looking infected......bloody biatching thing.

16th Jan 2015
Saw Dr Parmar for a check over today for the first time since the op
Not bad as meetings with Doctors go.
He's pleased with the operation and the chest stability which is fab
The lung will not get any better until I have another operation to pin it open
Then only marginally ...So out of breath a lot then in the future.
That worries me but I will learn to breath better with the one I have left of course proving them damn wrong oh yes infuckingdeedee
However, Bob the bastard cancer is a Thymic Carcinoma which I thought was the better option than Lung cancer but which wasn't quite as good as I had hoped .
So it's chemo time for Pillagius
In my mind I thought I may get away with just radiotherapy
I'm OK with it all as that's the way it is .. I was hoping in my heart for no chemo and the lung would improve more but fuck it I'm alive .. and still bloody handsome !

As it transpired I never had to have chemo and with the knowledge I have gleaned then I have to say I NEVER will…EVER. This is my decision based on my research. The truth is simple. It's my journey and the thought of going through that dreaded treatment fills me with the highest level of fear. I will take my chances elsewhere.

17th Jan 2015

"How are you?'
It's an innocent enough question, but one I've come to dread. Here's the problem. After a few months of being in the cancer club, I'm starting to lose track of whom I have told and whom I haven't. It's not that I've made any great secret of the fact, quite the opposite. In most respects the more people who know the easier it is for me, but it's really not that much fun telling people. Particularly people I know and like.
So here's the thing.
When someone says "How are you?" I'm not sure if they're really saying:
"Hi, I heard all about the (whispered) 'you-know-what.' Dreadful business. How's the treatment going? How's Sarah holding up? Where does it hurt? What's chemo like? Can I see your scar? How come your hair hasn't fallen out? Is there anything I can do? Etc, etc."
Or:
"How are you?
By the way before you launch into a lengthy and potentially embarrassing answer, can I just point out that this is an entirely rhetorical question, I am blissfully unaware of your current medical predicament, and frankly only ask because it is the socially accepted way to greet someone I haven't seen for a while. I have no real interest in the minutia of your probably tedious and uneventful life, so why don't I just say "Mustn't

grumble" and reciprocate by asking about their wife and kids, and where we went for the summer holiday."

You see the problem?

The potential for awkwardness here is considerable. Do they know or don't they? Are they just not mentioning the elephant in the room out of politeness, or because they haven't spotted it yet?

To take the easy way out – "Never been better thanks!" seems disingenuous and of course is a fucking lie and therefore rather goes against the grain. On the other hand just blurting out "Fine thanks, apart from the small matter of the grapefruit sized tumour called Bob that could well kill me that lurks in my chest cavity. Actually I did say that just the once. I'm not proud of it. It was at a party, and it was to someone who I don't particularly like, who was drunk and just wouldn't shut up. So when he finally stopped talking about his tawdry, awful life, finally took a breath and another swig of his Bacardi Breezer and enquired after mine. I told him straight. It certainly shut him up, but using my disease as a weapon was a low trick. I've resolved never to do it again. The C Card does rule though.

So, what to do?

Well I find the pre-emptive strike works well. "Hi! How are YOU?"

"Absolutely bloody terrible. Life is hardly worth living?"

(In a concerned tone.) "Really? I'm very sorry to hear that. Has one of your major organs failed? Has your homeland been overrun with fundamentalist Islamic extremists? Or maybe one of your children has a crack habit and joined the Catholic Priest Party Club? Don't tell me you picked up Necrotizing Faciitis from a dirty teaspoon?"

"No but the traffic on the bridge was an absolute bitch. Forty-five minutes to get to the office. Some wanker spilt coffee on my Armani shirt, and I've lost the key to my locker at the gym."

FIRSTWORLDFUCKINGPROBLEMS .com
"Oh! you poor lamb. I see what you mean. How do you go on?
Life can deal us some cruel blows sometimes can't it? What you
need is a nice cup of tea and a lie down."
Pilly rant over (and partly nicked from the wonderful C Word
book)

17th Jan 2015
"Chemo...recreational drugs for warriors"
That's the new t shirt chaps with a great big WOOF on the back
!!
I am about to order CHEMO -Recreational drugs for a Pillage T-
shirt......brilliant.
Its 5.23pm. I had two Paracetamols at 5.50am this morning.
That's all the pain killers I've had today. Bloody pleased .....
hard as nails bloke !!
Hey mon amies...
People keep on saying that I am an inspiration and that is
really kind. However, I'm really not. I have cancer and I am
trying to fight the bloody thing. My odd sense of tumour
humour made me call the cancer Bob. That's a little odd maybe
but certainly not inspirational eh!!
I can either succumb to it or beat it. That is not inspirational
that's a choice. I chose for mainly altruistic reasons, to share
my journey both good and bad with you, my friends on here.
That's not inspirational that's me relying on your energy to
keep me sane and getting me through some rough times. I have
not doubt that there will be some shit ones to come...I get that.
So as I see it YOU lot ARE the inspirational ones, I am just a
mere mirror of that.
You are the ones giving the energy, the love, the support and I
could not be more grateful. So thank you. All the visits from
you wonderful people, all the phone calls, texts, pm's, pictures

etc have helped me in a million ways.

I had my operation six weeks ago. Tomorrow morning I am driving myself to Birmingham airport and I am attending a martial arts lesson by my fellow zipper club member the TRULY INSPIRATIONAL Eddie Quinn. I will be able to do very little but I will be there cos I am alive and that's what I do ..... I intend to live the rest of my life as well as I can. That's six fucking weeks after MAJOR SURGERY...of that I am proud.....but its down to you reprobates and the tender ministrations of Mrs. P, who frankly has been amazing. She is the one who has put me to bed watching me scream in agony and wiped away the tears. She has pushed and prodded to make sure I stay positive. She has let me have a little insight into the person I have to evolve into and I cannot thank her enough for that. That's the very best I can give myself and to the world around me.

21st Jan 2015

I have had a text tonight of great magnitude. I am most honored and thrilled to be asked to do this but it may be a secret ..... so I won't say anything .....but BLOODY HELL .... HOW COCKING COOL and it happens in June. Better bloody stay alive for this bad boy eh !!

22nd Jan 2015

Has just been kicked in the balls. Got back from Doctors not only does he think my pain from yesterday is kidney stones but also he showed me the letter to the Oncologist from the histology department and it appears that Bob is particularly aggressive, much more so than I thought.

I've been so positive I think over this but feel deflated and beaten up at the moment really badly. In Spartacus terms .... Jupiter has firmly stuffed cock up arse.

In truth I'm sitting here in tears and feel devastated to my very core. I will pick myself up shortly because that's what I do. Thank you all ... my aging noddle is in a complete spin at the moment, so if I seem distant or don't answer you immediately then please forgive me. Need to clear my head and get it straight. Not in a great place so will do some should searching on my own for a bit

I've had a few hours of head clearing and thinking. I'm back and smiling. Thank you all for your love and best wishes. Feel stronger and even though my balls are still hurting I am now in a reasonable place xx

I'm actually feeling blessed...thank you my friends for all the phone calls and messages. You have no idea as to how much everyone helps at a time like this

Namaste xx

23rd Jan 2015
Well I have to say I am feeling a bit more positive and have got my head in a much better place this morning. Just a shock yesterday from the high I was on I guess. Also the balls are feeling a bit less tender from the tablets the Doc gave me. Damn you kidney stones ... "thou shalt not pass Wizard" he says in best Gandalf voice in head. Much love to all the people who helped so much in my dark time yesterday. Has anyone got a water distiller I could buy or borrow please?

24th Jan 2015
Early start on Sunday....BIG SCAN DAY to see where the bastard cancer has regrown after the operation. Bit nervous if honest...but hey ho

25th Jan 2015
I had my scans today and the injected dye stuff. Have been to

Leicester and had to come home much earlier as I was so tired. Now I need a bit of advice please. I came out of hospital fifty days ago which is fifty six after the operation. Bearing in mind I have no right lung now what sort of position should I be looking at for myself. Should I be pleased where I am or should I try a bit harder ...I have no baseline to gauge it against. Thanks chaps for all the lovely wishes btw

26th Jan 2015
Up and about to go to Warwick to spend time with a Respiratory Therapist can't breathe very well lets get that changed soon eh
At last some good news
Back from Physio. Her words Mr. Pillage you are a walking bleeding miracle (they actually weren't but that was the gist). Apparently someone my age will be very breathless from such a severe operation for up to twelve weeks after surgery, let alone with the collapse of the lung and being such a long term smoker. There is a little air going into the top part and I did VERY well on my oxygen saturations after and during exercise. She's showed me some exercises and I have to say I feel a lot better and more positive with the potential outcome of at least this part of the journey!!

28th Jan 2015
Can anyone help me with advice on benefits. I have never claimed a penny in my life, but realise I am pretty much dead wood at the dojo for a while at least. Let alone with the treatments looming. Is there any support I can get hold of as I think after 32 years working full-time it's about time I got something back.
(*I didn't get a penny by the way as I didn't follow through on this one*).

This was a bad day, a very, very bad day. One that I chose to keep back from the world. I think probably as I did not want to admit to myself. I went to the doctors about a couple of things and he spoke to me frankly about the prognosis after getting all the test results back. Six months left for me. I was devastated beyond measure. However the first thing that went through my mind was 'fuck it lets prove him wrong'. I planned to have a party on the 29th July. You see if I had gone six months and one day then I had won. Told you I was odd eh? You really have no idea as to what it feels like to get this sort of prognosis. I still find it hard to discuss as it was so painful and mentally debilitating. I decided that day I wasn't going to die during that time framework. Once again my belligerent nature served me magnificently.

31st Jan 2015
I re watched this video with some pride this morning...possibly one of the three greatest nights of my life. The last class I taught before we even knew if BOB was operable. It was and I said my goal was to be back on the mats in 3 months (so by 16th Feb). I have been already and managed 6 lengths jogging up and down the dojo.
I am alive
I am strong
and I am FABULOUS (until the chemo!!)
BUT STILL SMILING xx
Thanks again to all who took part that wonderful evening

This video being a wonderful piece of work by Richard Barnes, and was the edited final cut of the film he had made of my last night teaching at the dojo and set to my favourite Elbow track. As I said earlier one day like this a year will see me right.

2nd Feb 2015
It's two months today I was being wheeled down to the
surgeon. In that two months I have not only survived but I
have thrived. The pain at times has been horrendous, the
mental ups and downs have been awful, the prognosis's
offered from brilliant to well let's not go there eh.
However I look back and cannot thank you lot from the bottom
of my heart for all the good wishes, visits and love. As my Doc
said last week you are only at the start of this journey and of
course I am scared with the Oncologist visit not far off. No
doubt the chemo will be horrendous but I will get through.
BOB you little bastard time to go soon my friend.
Talking of friends..... it's amazing how some SO CALLED people
have been conspicuous in their absence of support. You know
who you are (most owe me money)...when I am better
MrFuckingKarmabus will be paying a visit. You are hereby
warned….

8th Feb 2015
I write tonight with a slightly heavy heart if I am true to myself.
Tomorrow is now dawning and my little protective bubble is
about to end. I meet with the Oncologist at 12pm and I will
then know basically what the rest of my life will entail. Frankly
I am shitting gold ones.....especially after the comment from my
GP two weeks ago. Whatever happens I hope I meet it with
courage and dignity.... an attribute not often associated with
me!!
This weekend though has been an awesome and totally
memorable one...and it has worked out I have been busy for
most of it surrounded by friends who I love dearly. Friday
grand Rugby adventures with Richard Barnes Mike Knight and
Graham Wendes all dear dear people and philosophers all.
Saturday at a truly wonderful book launch with the eclectic

Andy Gibney and lovely to see Elizabeth Pickford after many years .. Great event well done and then today going to the Master Alfie Lewis and Donna Lewis tournament in Rugby . Always the best of times to see my friend mentor and martial arts legend Steve Rowe accompanied by the unique force of nature that is Russell Jarmesty. Finished off tonight with a trip to see the film Selma about the civil rights movement with Martin Luther King.

Amongst this have been numerous calls wishing me well including one from China from the ginger love god Ian Goehler. Thank you all so very much.

I need to dig deep right now so if any of you have a little spare healing and positive energy Mr P could do with a little right now.

Namaste xx

I've also decided to walk the Pennine Way to raise money for Macmillan Nurses with Bob Sykes in August. Someone needs to keep him in order eh !!. Me, Bob, Bob, one lung mountains...what on earth could possibly go wrong !!

So far this has not transpired. It may yet do in the future, but a Bob or two can be contrary.

9th Feb 2015

Just out ....there is good news and bad news. The cancer is called Thymic Carcinoma (not Bob) and is an extremely aggressive little so and so. They showed me the pre op scans and Jesus fucking Christ it was a big one (that's what she said !!!!!!!) they are going to start radio therapy very quickly and have 30 sessions booked. The bad news is that as a by-product, the one remaining lung is likely to get damaged and will result in permanent tissue death (Pulmonary Fibrosis). Means I will be seriously fucked breathing even more. They will then look at chemo after this to mop up any residue as it may have gone into my lymph glands.

12th Feb 2015
PLEASE TAKE NOTICE
I NEED SOME HELP please and some serious thinking by you guys. I have been talking to a fabulous guy and fellow martial artist a Mr. Paul Coleman who sadly is also suffering from the dreaded Cancer and things don't look that good. We have talked long and hard and although he is taking many of the remedies I am banking on from a holistic standpoint, it seems to be getting worse. He has a three year old son and at present not looking at seeing him reach his fifth birthday. My own BOB isn't too great either I feel so I need your help. I need to raise approximately £4000 to fund a really extreme therapy for myself and Paul. It has to be raised relatively quickly. I am thinking crowd funding or something similar but am open to any ideas. I am willing to do more or less anything to raise this for him.

12th Feb 2015
I go to bed with the lovely feeling that we have raised £730 on a Just Giving Page I set up since this afternoon for mine and Paul's treatment. Thank you all feeling genuinely blessed xxx

13th Feb 2015
Day 1 complete and we have raised nearly £1100 how fabulous xxxx

15th Feb 2015
This is the start of another testing week. Three hospital appointments back to back then the start of the radiotherapy. 30 sessions in 30 days ... the idea is to nuke the cancer. The by -

product is lung destruction...an organ I seem to have very little left of anyway. This actually frightens me, as I couldn't catch my breath today on occasion. Still a productive week and nearly £1300 raised to help myself and Paul, so thank you one and all. All in all I am in good auspices and have spoken to the Right Rev Scott Caldwell for the first time. I am still alive and the cancer don't scare me much after talking to him!! I hope you all have a fantastic week.

16th Feb 2015
A good session today with my respiratory Physio. Healing is good though oxygen saturation levels are a little down. Never bloody realised the broken ribs will probably take 7-8months to heal and will be bloody painful. All good and smiling though.

18th Feb 2015
Good news and bad news. I've got lurgie for the first time since the operation. This is going to be interesting to try and stop me getting pneumonia in the collapsed lung. With afore mentioned lurgie I have had to sit doing breathing tests for an hour and a half in a special container that's air tight. Not at all pleasant I promise you. The good news is the nurse asked to do the tests as he is a martial artist and is a fan of my stuff. That was cool. Sore throat, cough temp and really bad feeling skin...great its MANFLU.... call the Ambulance, I am poorly.
If I don't make it until morning, you've all been amazing. Oh and BTW I am getting phone calls telling me that someone is using my cancer to bolster their own agenda. Please don't as it has REALLY fucked me off and I have had a lot of respect for you. If you make a mockery of what I and many others are going through then you sir are a class 1 TWAT.

19th Feb 2015
Plague Infection Day 2: Day 1 was a struggle after the seemingly benign cold I had on Day Zero mutated into the mother of all snot monsters and crept into my chest, nearly drowning me over night and nearly causing me to cough up a lung. Now that I'm on Day 2 of the plague infection I can barely speak, but when I do it sounds like a cross between Darth Vader and a vacuum cleaner. Mucus production has stepped up a gear today and I expect much bubbling and squeaking during the next twelve hours.
Now a lot of you are thinking this Pillage geezer ain't up to this big Pennine Walk in August. I hereby will tell you that as long as I am not on Chemo I will do it. My aim is the lot not just the 100 miles, if I have to do ten steps and rest I will do it. Why I hear you ask. I tell you ...... cos I can !. I need to push myself one last time and to do that with friends and other martial artists is one hell of a way to do it.
I ask my friends who REALLY know me ...will I do it ?
One week in and already up to £1477 that's nearly a third of the way there. Please donate even if its a £1.....if not Ill come back and haunt ya...naked.

21st Feb 2015
I'm so pissed off
All the coughing has re broken 2 of my ribs
I'm getting bored of being ill
That's two and a half months of pain no breathing and being a bit bloody useless

23rd Feb 2015
Am glad this weekend is out of the way. The truth is the cough I have has made me feel like I've been water boarded for forty eight hours. It's really scary when you cannot get enough air in

to stop you panting even when at rest. Not something I want to go through EVER again but I guess every time I get a cold now it's going to attack the weakened lungs. Not good at all. Apart from that I have to teach today for three hours ... my first since November. It's going to be fun

24th Feb 2015
I said at the last class I taught in November that I would be back on the mats by the end of Feb. I taught for three hours yesterday as well as today, AND IT FELT REALLLLLLLY GOOD. My thanks to everyone, for helping over this difficult time. but that is the ethos and spirit we have built over the past 12 years at the club. Our birthday is on the 3rd/3/03 so a time that is looming quickly. We will be celebrating this auspicious time with the biggest party EVER at the dojo this Sat with the wonderful *Watchsnatchers.*
I wonder often as to what we have achieved and done over the past decade and I haven't the time or the typing skills to do it justice. It was almost epitomised by a post on a thread from earlier. It sort of goes like this about GKR Karate.

Craig Galvin
It must be that time of year again for them.
I had two of their " instructors " call to my house the other day, they gave me some spiel about feeling confident, safe, empowered and said above all I could pay in installments and said I could sign my kids up to help them grow in confidence.
The weirdest thing happened, I said:
"IF, I was going to sign my children up anywhere, with any instructor it would be with someone whom has a reputation for teaching quality. "
Their reply:
" Oh, quality is what we are known for ".

The following sort of slipped out:

" No, I'm sorry, you misunderstand me, I meant Anthony Pillage at the Way of the Spiritual Warrior, he is a great bloke, great classes and his reputation stands on its own merits. "

All they said after that was:

"Oh, erm, Yes ok. I am sorry to have bothered you ".

If I didn't know better, I'd say they may have heard of you Tony LOL..!!

It made me laugh like a drain and I thank Craig for sharing. Myself and Sarah defied all the odds time and time again to make WOTSW happen. This weekend some of the greatest martial artists EVER in the UK are gracing us with their presence at our charity seminar. If you can gauge a man's character by his friends then frankly I am FUCKING AWESOME. My bubble will be bursting soon with the onset of intense radiotherapy and then chemo if the radio is unsuccessful, which if I am honest I am totally frightened of. Please I beg of you lot of reprobates keep the energy and good vibes flowing when I am down as I no doubt will be. You have all been magnificent and my very soul has been enriched by the hundreds of messages, pm's, posts, texts etc. I could not find words to express my gratitude to each and every one of you. Namaste fellow travellers.

2nd March 2015

I am a bit tired this morning so my wax ain't too lyrical and I have a few breathing issues to deal with.

However, I look back at one of the most amazing weekends possible at The Warriors Assemble. I will write longer later as I need to thanks about a 1000 people but what I will say is this. The instructors who graced the mats were gentlemen and of the finest calibre. The attendees gave 100 % throughout, The Watchsnatcher's gig was awesome and we got about 50 people onto the Blood Cancer Donor register. You were all amazing. Thank you.

I also managed to complete another two off my bucket list. I believe I have had at the dojo EVERY instructor of note that I have ever wanted to train with at my dojo except for Mr. Maurice Teague and Trevor Roberts. This was completed over the weekend all we need now is Kelly S. Worden and I've had the lot. Both Mo and Trevor set in my opinion the standard of what I love about martial arts. Gentlemen it was an honor..... thank you

6th March 2015

OK I've had a think and it's this. As I've lost a lung now would that be enough to start looking at the next special Olympics ... I fancy that. Just need something I am vaguely good at. Richard Barnes is there one lung squash or what about special adaptive TKD that might do...any thoughts appreciated.

10th March 2015

Oh and I taught my first adult class last night since the op
To be fair I was truly bloody magnificent !!
Well here goes
Back to the gym today for the first time since October
Bit apprehensive but what the hell
Still no news from the bloody cancer department about the start of my treatment
Also time to take stock and move onwards and upwards

12th March 2015

Really struggling today mentally
Very hard to keep positive all the time
Truth is I'm currently scared to bits and as I'm not in any great pain currently I sometimes forget what's going on inside me.

Then I remember but keeping busy and getting on with stuff
and work keeps my mind occupied
Then BAM when the real world hits it hits like Rocky Balboa
through a thin focus mitt
Chased the radiotherapy department for the start of my
treatment, a treatment which will cause pain and destroy part
of the good lung
One I can just about manage now with
I wish beyond measure that I wasn't here right now feeling as I
do
Sorry ... but I've promised my friends the truth as to what is
happening
Need some healing mon amie's please
Namaste xxxx
My thanks to you all today for your support and love. It's
helped enormously

13th March 2015
This poem is dedicated to Jack Bristow and Anthony Pillage.

Don't give up!
Some days are great, some days are awful.
Sometimes you are bursting with energy and happiness,
Sometimes you feel pain and depression.
Just for today, find the strength to keep going, don't worry
about tomorrow.
Try your best, just for today.
A Warrior should always train both mind and body.
Find peace within yourself and you can find peace more easily
with others.
Every day is training, training for yourself.
Though knockbacks and failures are possible, persevere, make
the best of today.

There is only today.
Then tomorrow try your best for that day.
Welcome each new day as an opportunity to do your best for that day.
Every day you try your best is a penny in your life bank.
Then one day you will be rich, simply because you never gave up and you tried your best.
Just for today.
- Anthony J. Bailey (Founder of Mizu Ryu Ju Jitsu)

13th March 2015
It looks like treatment starts this week ..... so many thanks to all the guys in the adult classes I have taught this week. It's been an absolute blast thank you

15th March 2015
I apologise to you lot but in truth I am totally struggling at the moment and everything is getting to me so if I'm not my normal self just bear with me. This next month is going to be extremely hard I think.

16th March 2015
I have cancer so life ain't brill
But Kanye Fucking West headlining GLAStonburY has just about finished me off FFS NOOOOOOOOOOOOOOO!!!!!! I'd rather wank off a grizzly bear than be exposed to that moron.

Radio Therapy?

17th March 2015

Tomorrow I start my radiotherapy at 12.10pm..... cannot tell you how nervous I'm starting to get. I've eaten clean this week and started my holistic plan for recovery.... shit just got real!!. Wish me well my learned compardres, IT'S SHOWTIME !!

18th March 2015

Got to the hospital and apparently the mapping was out as my chest has changed size so no go today...... they have to remap agghhhh

Basically when you have radiotherapy they tattoo dots on you to line up the huge zappy machine. As you can imagine cancer has a ravaging effect on you and your body shape. The dots MUST be in perfect alignment or the beam will miss its target, causing damage to healthy parts of the body but missing the cancer completely.

I still remember vividly the feeling of dread walking up to the doors of the Arden Cancer Centre. I had no idea of what was going to be in store. I stopped ten yards away, tears welling up in my eyes, as scared as I have ever been. The fear of the unknown and the sight of all these bald, terribly ill looking people coming from their treatments was too much. It took every ounce of my mental strength to go in and present myself. The waiting area was packed. All these poor people with cancer. Some looked as if they could barely rise to their feet. Surely this wasn't my future as well.

My breathing problems started when I had to lie down on the treatment bench. Not only was it extremely painful, but as soon as I was horizontal I couldn't breathe at all. The remaining phrenic nerve didn't seem to have the strength to power my good lung. This scared the absolute shit out of me as on more than one occasion I felt as if I would never be able to force any air into my lung ever again.

When they lay you onto the table you cannot move a muscle for normally about fifteen minutes. I had to quickly learn how to not panic, just take miniscule sips of air and hope that they would finish the process as quickly as possible. The staff here were not only extremely well trained but absolute angels. I could not praise them higher. They were going to become a major part of my life for the following six weeks.

So you have to imagine that you are laying on this multi-million pound hi-tech piece of technological equipment waiting to be radiated. You have to lie perfectly still as there is absolutely no margin for error, otherwise they will miss the cancer and destroy your remaining good cells. These people were absolutely amazing...it's all about angles and trigonometry, talking their strange radiographer language until they get it right. Then your bloody nose starts to itch but you cannot move a muscle. This place was going to be my home for the next six weeks of my life.

25th March 2015
Off to bed ...don't feel very good......end of day 3 radiotherapy.
It shouldn't be affecting yet but seems to be.

You see it's weird. I call it the radiotherapy dance. Day one you walk in, get on the bed and they do their stuff. You don't feel it, you don't smell it, all you do is hear it whirring and zapping. Blimey that was ok, not half as bad as I had feared and off you trot (or in my case a slow walk) back to the waiting room and back home. As you can see though by day three, I wasn't feeling too special.

You are allocated a daily time, mine was 12pm. There are four pods, each manned by 4-5 staff doing the radiotherapy treatments. On the other side of the building there are the chemotherapy suites. As people had a set time we got to recognize the same faces and were soon on nodding terms with many. I have always been a great studier of the human condition and sitting in the waiting room provided a wonderful opportunity to do just that. Day one people are walking in quite sprightly. By the end of the first week that speed had slowed down considerably.

By the end of week two I had slowed down yet again. Week four was my worst; I could hardly put one leg in front of the other. I remember going to see my Pulmonary Nurse at Warwick and had to literally pull myself along the corridor by the handrail. She took one look at me and sent me home. I was also having huge, huge problems eating; a common factor for people having radiotherapy. I remember clearly, shuffling round Tesco's in Coventry and literally finding nothing I could stomach, even after the second trawl around its lengthy food aisles. My diet was consisting of Fortisips given by the dietician at the hospital, Lucozade and wine gums. The wine gums oddly were the only things that didn't make me gag. So in affect I'm putting complete shit inside me, all sugary based products which are doing little to nourish me but fucking loads to nourish young Bob.

And therein lies another problem. This extreme diet meant I was losing weight rapidly, as well as any muscle tone that had been left. So, during this time my treatment became far more difficult as it sometimes took the nursing staff fifteen, maybe even twenty minutes to line up the tattoos. They would literally knead your flesh to get the position exactly right. As you can imagine I was not the only one having these problems. What really got to me was when this knock on effect meant you may have got in for your appointment thirty minutes to an hour late. People would sit in reception moaning about they weren't being seen exactly on time. Fuckheads the lot of them, ignorant thundertwonks. You would also have the problem that each week one of the machines would have to be calibrated, putting pressure on the other three pods. However, whatever was thrown at the staff they responded magnificently and my respect for them just grew and grew.

28th March 2015
After day five I feel like I've got REALLY bad flu onset !!
I'm beaten at 8.52pm off to bed I feel dreadful. Shivering, in loads of pain, can't breathe and frozen to my core...haven't felt this rough since the week after the operation......
Loads of breathing problems this morning
Panic attacks and the like
Very scary

31st March 2015
I am now seven sessions down out of thirty. I feel about 1 out of 10 and its gonna get a hell of a lot worse, I know that. They don't really prepare you for this and as ever mine has to be a difficult one. My thanks to Andy Gibney for his visit today to help get my head right about my breathing......
There is no doubt that the support and love of my friends has helped beyond all measure. Seriously if you have a friend or

relative who is going through cancer and its medical procedures I implore you give them a call, or just pop and say hi and show that you care. Sometimes just those few words can make the world of difference to someone.

The honesty is I don't seem to have a lot of reserves left at the moment so if I'm not about on here or whatever it's because I am exhausted and resting.

WWWWWWWWWWWWWWWWWWWWWWWWTTTTTTTTTTT TTTTTTTTTFFFFFFFFFFFFFFF is going on I feel like death

Please note that there is an enormous gap in the posts at this stage. Why? Because I was far too ill from the radiotherapy to even vaguely write a word in nearly three weeks. I can't really remember much from this time apart from feeling like I had the worst flu ever coupled with stabbing pains throughout my body. The radioactive nuclear bomb had exploded and then some. This was the fallout.

Jack Bristow and the Stroke of Doom 25th April

Martial Artists Supporting Jack Bristow

The Warrior known as Jack Bristow has inspired some of the best Martial Arts Instructors around the UK to support his cause for raising funds and awareness for Piam Brown Children's Cancer Ward

Book on this exciting seminar from some of the best Martial Arts Instructors in the UK

Mick Tully, Tony Bailey, Anthony Pillage, Lucci Del-Gaudio, Len Dunce, Brian Bossett, Lindsey Andrews, Rocci Williams, Ron Peploe, Peter Holmes, Anthony Masters, Clare Brown, Roberto Almeida, Paul Hamilton, Bryan Andrews___

Regional, British, European & World Champions all coming to Basingstoke to support Jack Bristow in his fight against cancer.

*Pressure Points * Weapons Combat * Modern Ju Jitsu * Kickboxing * Street Combatives*
* Self Defence * MMA * Judo * Traditional Ju Jutsu * Brazilian Jiu Jitsu * Karate *

Junior Day Pass £25 - Senior Day Pass £35

A collector's booklet of all Instructor profiles is available FREE to all attendees

Jnrs 11am-4.30pm Sat 25th April 2015
Snrs 11am-5pm Sunday 26th April 2015

Shin Gi Tai Martial Arts Academy, Basingstoke. RG22 4BA

ALL proceeds go to support the Piam Brown Children's Ward and Jacks family.
We take nothing and all instructors and venues are giving their time & services for FREE.

Contact:- seminar@mizuryu.co.uk to book a place NOW

In conjunction with

Martial Artists Supporting Children With Cancer   Basingstoke Ju Jitsu Club   Shin Gi Tai Martial Arts Academy

Tony Bailey had called me and told the story of one of his students, Jack Bristow. Jack had taken a kick in the balls playing football. The pain wouldn't subside so his Mum and Dad took him to see the doctors. After tests they found that he had testicular cancer. They operated and also gave him chemo (I believe that he was the first child in the world to have this double procedure).

Throughout the pain of the chemical induced hell he remained upbeat and the Basingstoke club Shin Gi Tai decided to give a fundraiser on Jacks behalf.

I was asked to come and teach, which of course was my first time teaching a seminar since late November the previous year. I also probably hadn't driven more than ten miles; this was one hundred and five.

I thought that it would be a great idea to do some "Batman" fighting based on the whole Keysi / Defence Labs system that had been used in the previous three Batman films. If honest I always had wanted a Batman outfit (what man if they told the truth wouldn't). So a day later Amazon had delivered the suit. It was awesome apart from the fact that the abdominal muscle molding rather negated any movement whatsoever and made the whole idea especially awkward because of the soreness of my scar.

I arrived; got dressed and let some of the kids see me. Of course I found it tricky to move let alone teach in the get up, so I did a lot of what may be described as swooping.

The seminar went really well and as ever I thoroughly enjoyed the whole process of being back on the mats. I was totally

exhausted and decided to get home early. I got in the car, drove a few miles and felt dizzy, had pins and needles in my arm and leg and a severe weakness in my feet. Luckily there was a service station so I pulled in and had a cup of tea. Little did I know what had actually transpired was I had had a mini stroke or TIA. As ever the British universal drug of choice, TEA, was the miracle cure I needed. Too much bloody swooping I guess. It wasn't until later I realised just how very lucky I had been.

Just A Little Stroke

26ᵗʰ April 2015
The Awards Ceremony.
The MAI Awards are held up in Burton On Trent. I had won yet another meaningless certificate but had nominated a few close friends so wanted to go and support them. Luckily I was driven up there but due to what had happened the previous day I couldn't walk very well so I broke out my Canemaster fighting walking stick that Mark Shuey had presented me with a few years previously. I could barely hobble around but it was still amazing to see so many old friends and acquaintances. There is nothing really to say about the evening apart from at one point I was approached by someone who used to be a friend but had turned into a back stabbing wanker. He came over all smiles and bon homie and asked after my health. My reply was somewhat acerbic if honest. 'If you don't fuck off right now I'm going to smash the fuck out of you in front of the assembled four hundred people.' He left. In truth I was glad, as to be brutally honest I could hardly even stand let alone fight a Fifth Dan black belt... but I felt mentally good at sticking up for my principles, Well done you Mr. P, well played indeed.

27ᵗʰ April 2015
Ok medical bods a question
I am on Ondesterone for my nausea
On Saturday the left hand side of my face went sort of pins and needly and a bit numb just as I was setting off back from Basingstoke as well as weakness in my legs.

I pulled over for an hour until it passed
I also have slight pins and needles in my left arm I noticed today a very low level sort of tingling in that area and near my eye. Any ideas or should I go to the docs about it.

The thing about the radiotherapy is that it is cripplingly challenging and then some. Complete nausea, exhaustion, pain, headache, loss of all appetite and worst of all the feeling of utter helplessness. I have taken more than my share of 'A' class substances in my youth and this was like the world's worst come down after seventy-two hours awake. I kid thee not. What I hadn't realized is that I had had a stroke on the Saturday. Doh! I pulled over for a cup of tea for an hour and then went home. The amount of people who responded to this message was incredible. Included was a trauma doctor from the Czech Republic who suggested that I should take myself off to A & E immediately.

28th April 2015
Morning all..... admitted to hospital last night, they think I may have had a stroke so they have put me in the Oncology ward.
Still here
Very tired as poor man next to me having chemo has been sick all night
However, I give thanks for being me this beautiful morning
I spoke to loads of people here including people with terminal outcomes NOT ONE OF THEM I REPEAT NOT ONE OF THEM had done any research into helping or treating themselves outside of what their medical team had told them, all blindly just putting their trust in modern medicine. One man has been fighting cancer for five years. He was thirteen stone, went on chemo and down to six in only seven weeks. Just accepting his death in a very short time. They have all given up and accepted their lot meekly. Not one knew about any holistic treatments,

diet, oil or anything that would help themselves. It isn't the acceptance of death as inevitable, it's the complete giving up of the sanctity of life that I am appalled by if honest. You would think they would research and try to at least give themselves a better chance. I explained the path I have taken, they have been amazed and all of a sudden a little spark of life showed in their eyes again. I am a fighter I will beat this or at least die fighting. We need to educate the sheeples.... Pillage on a mission to give some hope to those with none left. All my friends on here who have this fucked up disease are doing everything possible to live thrive and survive, I am proud of you pioneers and warriors all. Let's fucking well show this disease who we are and that we take no crap. Also so many thanks for all the calls and messages yesterday. One love people xx

29th April 2015

Lisa Lynch, in her blog 'A Right Tit' *made me laugh when she mentioned* Who wants to be a millionaire? *The person on it then gets through to the final and has a cancer based question and she would volunteer as the phone a friend role. That's exactly how I felt as there was a steady stream of patients coming to my bed to ask questions about holistic treatment protocols.*

30th April 2015

GORDONS ALIVEEEEEEEEEEEEE

Well big day for me...out of hospital and just agreed that Lee Charles will play me in the upcoming biopic film of my life. Tough decision between him or Denzil Washington.... well done mate. I sense Golden Globes awaiting !!

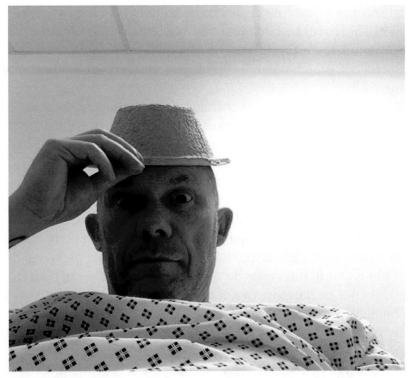

HELPPPPPPPPPP
Anyone free at 12.15 on Friday to take me to hospital. Please I
will sing and entertain you or offer a neck massage
Just got back from UCH again. I had another bad turn this
morning which they think was a Transient Ischaemic Attack
(TIA) or "mini stroke" My left foot and leg has lost strength and
face numb. Two weeks of doing nothing but rest. I WILL GO
INSANE please entertain me good people xx

1st May 2015
I've been awake since 4am cogitating. Over many years lots of
people have strongly suggested I write a book on my life. In
recent months and telling people the one thing you don't have

is time and now realising just how true that is I have decided to do it. There will be two versions, one to be published now pretty much warts and all. The second after I shuffle off this mortal coil which will tell you exactly where the bodies are buried !!

The title is this "PILLAGE or tonight I supped from the moat of Castle Depravity". I have a story to tell now I believe worthy of telling and all proceeds will help fund my future cancer projects. Those of you who have known me for years will understand my statement. I have had an amazing and truly interesting life and maybe a little wisdom I have gained over my fifty-three years may help people. There will be some stories that you will not believe. I will share being homeless, the drug years, my martial journey, the highs, the partying, the despair. Out of interest who would actually bother to read it?

I could not be more in awe of the medical staff at the University College Hospital over the past 6 weeks and of course during my time there after my operation. They do an amazing job with great fortitude and humour and care. I have spoken to the powers that be there and we are offering a THREE MONTH FREE Pass to anyone who works there in whatever capacity and there kids. This will be officially done early next week.

Well that's it now 30 days of intense radiotherapy now finished thank goodness. Apparently it will hit me like an express train in about 2 weeks but the nausea and sickness should be on the wane within 10 days so that's something to look forward to. Again thanks so much to all the people who have run me about and of course Sarah who has done the majority of mopping the brow and the driving. The truth is I would say in many respects this has been harder to get through than the operation. Just say a few prayers to your god that it has worked as I can't see me doing chemotherapy EVER!!

2nd May 2015

Radiotherapy. One of my mums' is an occupational health worker for Macmillan in the Oncology ward of UCH. I remember clearly when she asked what my treatment programme was I told her a course of 30. What was the spacing she enquired? Daily I said. The look she gave me was one I would describe as this. You are reversing down your drive...you run over a very small puppy and it's the look in your eyes as you watch it whimper and bleed to death in your arms. She didn't say a word though. She came in to visit me in hospital and gave me a hug. I said "*I know why you gave me that look now*". She smiled and that was enough. I was just pleased it wasn't chemo as the first option. So went into it blissfully unaware of just how hard it would be. Some days, even before the stroke thing, I could hardly walk, no energy, blindingly bad nausea and sickness, memory failure all sorts. So a few questions to fellow sufferers. How long does it take for your taste and smell to return to a normal state? Mine seems 10x more intense and extremely skewed. Normal household smells make me feel so sick it's unbelievable.

2nd May 2015

Oh and in my quiet week I also invented a new phrase (well my crap spelling and not checking did) Instead of Tickety Boo meaning all well and dandy I came up with Rickety Boo the same thing but when you are not feeling very well. I hope this catches on

4th May 2015

I'm struggling today
Legs as weak as a weak thing
That'll teach me for dancing yesterday

Badly but still dancing
Got to take those small battles eh chaps x
I'm feeling brave enough to watch last night's drama The C-Word starring Sheridan Smith
It looks like an amazing piece of work and a true story of a woman's fight against breast cancer
I hate predicting emotion but I think I may well be shedding a few tears later.
Wow just wow
The insightful accuracy of her emotions is unbelievable
This is a truly incredible piece of work
She calls the tumour The Bullshit
Mine was Bob
I wonder what other people called theirs
You have to find those times where sometimes you forget you have cancer
I just saw the lady come up to her after the wedding and discuss what was going on
Fuck me it's like the MAI awards
I cannot believe how accurate this is compared to what's happened to me
I can relate 1000000000000%
I can't stop the tears as its sometimes so hard to make people understand what is going on in your head. This is the first time I have seen anything that has even vaguely come close to explain what goes through you during the Cancer Journey.

5th May 2015
The decision has been made. The book you are all asking for will be the charting of the journey from last Oct when I was first diagnosed with cancer. It may be interesting to men as we have seen the wonderful interpretation of *The C Word* on T.V. which charted a woman's perspective with breast cancer. The

working title as a homage to that brave lady and to Bob is The B Word!! Named after the little tinker ...but I need better. The project starts tomorrow as I have a great day planned with Paul Coleman and shenanigans afoot! It will be more intimate and more personal than what I have put up before and a lot of thoughts I haven't shared as yet. Who is in?

I seem to use, as others oft do, the word journey a lot when talking about what has gone on. I don't even like the word in this bloody context as it implies a pleasant trip or some life changing metaphysical experience. Cancer is not a fucking journey my friends, no siree Bob. Cancer is a neutron bomb dropped in the middle of your world exploding with unimaginable force and venom.

I am, in all honesty, paraphrasing a comment I read by Lisa Lynch here and she totally gets it right.
"Being diagnosed with cancer is like being told you've got twenty minutes to revise for an A level exam in a language you have never studied (Parlez Vous chemo?). You walk into your appointment assuming your cramming days are behind you and come out blinded by need to know, baffling terminology that's as unfamiliar as a snowman to a Fijian.

I'm after a favour. Is anyone going up to the Martial Arts Show this weekend that I could cadge a lift off of and share petrol costs or are insured and we could go in the mighty Hummer. I'm not sure I could drive that far at the moment even if it is only 90 miles
As soon as I am better I am going to buy a boat and live on it...any advice...... I will have a selection of nautical hats for visitors. NO IM NOT JOKING btw. Seriously any advice would be very welcome

6ᵗʰ May 2015

Back to work now. I'm doing a couple of hours at home than a couple manning the desk and being generally awesome at the dojo. I'm hoping to be back teaching a little next week if you'll have me xx

BTW guys I am seriously going to do my best to get up a visitor to The Martial Arts Show this weekend in Doncaster. I have cancelled my teaching slot's as I didn't want to let people down if I was poorly and I think after last week's strokes etc. that was wise!! However, my place has been taken by the martial arts monster that is Peter Holmes, a DSI instructor of the highest order and if you think points don't work then I urge you to train with this exceptional man.

Was looking at some pics. These pictures were taken 6 months apart. I can't believe the change...bloody cancer. I need to get back to my ruggedly handsome self quickly.

Six months earlier

7th April 2015

I am so angry it hurts. After months on inactivity I went in today to help with the polling station role that the dojo played. By 7pm after seven hours I was waning a tad. Then poor Sarah had to be taken home as she had nearly fainted. I was always going to lock up in case of trouble as the voting finishes at 10pm with a thirty min clean up time. I've had to lug things (which really fucked my chest), it was freezing as they had to keep all the doors open all day, I had to deal with morons and had to tell one of the Labour councilors sons if he didn't fuck off I would not be liable for my actions !! Arrogant little fucktard.

I have really hurt my chest moving stuff. I literally crawl into bed at 11pm only to be woken by the phone as one of the people running it had left a load of slips at the dojo that they needed or the WHOLE count was invalid. I've just got back. If I die in my sleep can someone wreak havoc on these bastards for me?

I'm actually really concerned I've done some serious damage to myself. If I hadn't of gone back the entire voting system of Coventry would have collapsed......

8th May 2015
Some fab news

Used a rewards spirometer, have to use it most days to see how my lungs go, haven't used it for a couple of weeks, when I had my first operation and I come out of hospital, I could get it up to around the 500 calibration mark, gradually over time I could reach it up to around 2000, the idea is to get it up to around 4000, and as a reward you get a little smiley face – today for the first time I got it to...3500! Things are on the up!

8th May 2015
I have just eaten the biggest meal for 6 months ... Homemade Spaghetti Bolognaise with a cheeky glass of Rioja.

I have my appetite back and its blooming marvelous

God that was incredible

There have been times over the past 2 months where I haven't managed to eat for 2 days sometimes because of the incredible nausea.

9th May 2015
I don't want to tempt fate. But don't I look brilliant in this pic. Really well compared to of late......THANK YOU

First time in 9 months I recognise myself

Felt vaguely human which was wonderful

9th May 2015
I really really have had the very best of days today even factoring in my alarm went off at 4.30 am and couldn't get back to sleep. My mate Peter Holmes had kindly driven from Peterborough to pick me up and take me home, as I wouldn't have been confident to drive so thanks bud.
As many of you are aware I have been involved heavily in other martial arts shows. So in truth tried not to have too many preconceptions regarding this event. It was in truth brilliant. Loads of great quality people, loads of audience, heaps of things going on and a tremendous energy.
I in truth have NEVER talked so much in my life. I will repeat this in case you think you've read it wrong... PILLAGE in truth have NEVER talked so much in my life
I would guess at least 200 people wanted to chat today and it was fucking lovely. People have been so kind in coming up and shaking my hand or hugging the crap out of me. Many total strangers who have been following my story and of course many friends. Everywhere I went I was asked for pictures or autographs. Believe me it was tremendous feeling to have been so aware on the effect this whole journey has had. I was honestly humbled. Five people pulled me to one side who have got people in their lives who are fellow cancer sufferers and told me how much my attitude has helped them ...that was the best bit by far. I honestly could not have expected such warmth and friendship as felt today. So thanks all so very much for making me feel so alive and happy.
On another tact I have enlisted the formidable entities of Alfie Lewis, Zara L Phythian   Peter Mogridge, Shaun Boland and John Burke into helping with the Disabled Martial Arts Awards and have spoken at length with Dave Lee and The

Adaptive Chaps led by Neil Kirkland (who are awesome) who are happy to support as well. Thanks again I'm pooped can't talk but if you are free tomorrow I honestly suggest to go up and have a look.

Sadly the second year didn't match up to the promise of the first!!

10th May 2015
When I had my stroke, I had a long chat with the senior nurse regarding the roadmap ahead of me. She was saying to me and Sarah, that in about 2 - 3 weeks the radiotherapy will hit like a steam train and lay me low for about 7 days. I know I was out and about yesterday but I am very, very sore today in my chest so maybe it's starting. I've been waiting for this to finish then I'm off to the Mediterranean on a cruise so let's get the next step over and done with.

10th May 2015
Mmmmm breathing back to shite level three and nausea back and now very sore chest internally!!
I think the nuclear explosion in my body is starting
Wish me luck chaps xx
I'm so fucked off I can't lie down again as I can't breathe when I do. Back out of bed and on the bloody computer so I can sit upright and gasp some oxygen, againaghhhhhh I thought I'd got over this shit

11th May 2015
Well in the words of Spartacus…. Jupiter has severely stuck cock up arse this morning. Been to the doctors. I have a growth on my back that has grown VERY rapidly and is in his words an

area of concern. Bloody marvellous ...off to see specialist on Wed they want to move that quickly. POOOOOOOOOOOOP

This was a peculiar sort of mole they eventually burnt off. The problem is that every ache and pain, every skin blemish, every feeling of illness reminds you and scares you that the cancer is back and spreading. It took me over a year to actually get my noggin around this.

11th May 2015
I taught an adult class tonight for the first time since the epic night in November
Bit rusty Bit sore Bit knackered
Bit brilliant
Thanks for the lovely welcome everyone x

13th May 2015
For some reason my post didn't go up. They are going to operate and remove little Bob sometime in the near future. She said it will scar my tattoo a bit...I pointed out my chest scar.......she shut up

14th May 2015
I have a feeling that the nuclear explosion is starting from the radiotherapy
I feel awful

14 May 2015
Yep it's time to tighten the chin straps
It's going to be a bumpy ride
They said that there would be a two, maybe three week gap between the end of giving me radiotherapy and the time it all culminates in destroying the rest of the cancer

They warned me it was going to be tough but Jesus its nuclear bomb explosion level of shite

15ᵗʰ May 2015
They said that when this hits my emotions will be shot to pieces....I feel like shit in the brain today so I guess it's here although I feel a little better. However I'll be doing FUCK all today.

You see whatever you do and wherever you go it's so hard to escape the wanky cancer. Bob is just as much a mental battle as it is a physical one. The medical powers that be, may know how to kill off tumours but there is little funded support to help repair shattered confidence, self-esteem and the fear of dying.

Macmillan are great though and were always supportive. I urge you don't give money to these cancer charities like the Race for Life Bollocks. The money is already within the big pharmaceutical bastard companies for a hundred years of research. Give your money to Macmillan as they are front line and were never lacking in my opinion in any way, shape or form. Getting your head in the right place to fight is the hardest thing for so many. I know from experience that you change from the very second you get the diagnosis. That's why I harp on about the extreme sanctity of friends and the love and support they offer; you need this more than anything.

15ᵗʰ May 2015
Just spoken to the hospital at some length. Apparently I am probably overdoing it and apparently my emotions and feeling shitty are to be totally expected. So if I act odder than normal I now at least have an excuse so please bear with me

17th May 2015
I feel like pooooooooooo again
Night xx

18ᵗʰ May 2015
Bloody hell, off to physio for my breathing. But god almighty I feel totally depressed and down...hate this

21ˢᵗ May 2015
Coventry Evening Telegraph
Anthony's sporting gesture to staff
10:00 21/05/2015

A Martial Arts expert is giving thanks to University Hospital staff that helped him through the fight of his life by offering free training at his centre.

Anthony Pillage, 53, had surgery to remove a large tumour from his chest just before Christmas and through the care from staff at University Hospitals Coventry and Warwickshire NHS Trust (UHCW), he returned to work just six weeks after the operation.

Anthony, a former Coventry Citizen of the Year and Coventry Sporting Hero, said: "After two and a half months of not knowing I had a lifesaving operation where they removed a tumour the size of a grapefruit. I lost my right lung, but I returned to work in six weeks.

"I am very grateful to everyone. They are absolutely excellent people who are always going beyond the call of duty.

"I have never gone through cancer before so it is really scary as to what happens. Now I am onto radiotherapy, every single one has been excellent, their patience has been amazing."

Anthony has decided to show his thanks by offering every staff member at UHCW, and their kids, to be able to train at his Way of the Spiritual Warrior Martial Arts Centre, in Foresthill, Coventry.

The World Martial Arts Hall of Fame Recipient said: "I am a great believer in putting back where possible so this is an open offer to anyone that works at the hospital or their family to come and train for three months for free as a thank you for their hard work helping me."

The offer doesn't just extend to his gym, as Anthony is also looking to offer free self-defence classes for medical staff at the hospital.

Anthony said: "In previous situations I have twice had to use my martial arts skills to help nurses with self-defence so I want to help by delivering a realistic self-defence class so that they can protect themselves should it ever come to do that.

"I would like to do this as a small gesture to thank everyone at the hospital."

21st May 2015
I feel the strongest today since last October what a wonderful feeling, seriously blessed

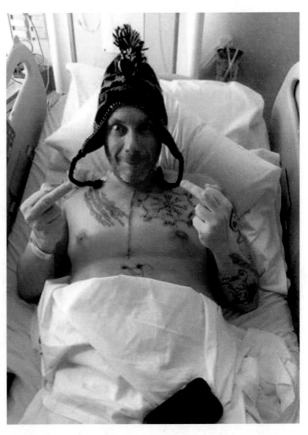

24th May 2015
I've just managed my first press up since the operation
How fucking cool is that
That's taken seven months to the day almost

10th June 2015
This is me in early December. Today I go off on a three week adventure culminating with watching The Who at Glastonbury. I couldn't even walk when this pic was taken..........Positive mind-set and great care plus gazillions of good friends has got me here today

12th June 2015

Today I had the unbelievable pleasure of having coffee on the harbour in Barcelona with a man who painted with Salvador Dali. Could one's life get any better?

14th June 2015 ·

The whole idea of my trip was to give me some much needed R&R after the past eight months of what has basically been hell.
I also wanted to do some serious thinking about life the universe and everything
I think there was also a bit of fuck it before I get my results in July and the possibility of the need for chemo looming
Sometimes I totally forget I have cancer and that is a good thing believe you me
I do feel stronger and when I think of me only five months ago shuffling up the street and being scared to lie down in case I couldn't breathe, I know I have done very very well
The first two days I wondered if I had done the right thing in being away for so long and in other countries.... I mean it's only 6 weeks ago I had a stroke for fucks sake and let's many travel insurance may not exactly stand scrutiny!! But in typical Pillage style thought that I could manage the trip
Now I know I have as my brain seems to be really kicking in again
Rome on the morrow
Now off for a tango class

Overdoing things

The Encounter
15th June 2015

Out of all the tales I can retell over this entire time comes today and has so many elements of what and who I am both in the spiritual, eclectic and belligerent parts of my psyche.

I am in my cabin and am awoken at about 3.40am by the people above me having a party to some very entertaining Salsa music. By 4.20am I am getting really pissed off but think these are people on holiday stop being such a grouchy bastard. But I then think, hang on there are many elderly people on the ship who I am sure wouldn't appreciate this level of noise at this time of the morning so I phone down to reception to see if they can sort it out...no bloody answer. I am now getting to the point of incandescence and decide to take matters firmly into my own hands. I get dressed and follow the sounds to cabin 1252 and knock sharply on the door. I was greeted by a very pissed Spanish looking guy, who didn't seem too concerned at my complaint. He went to shut the door in my face but I managed to block it with my foot. I am now literally beyond apoplectic. SO I barged my way in to the room where there was another two, also Hispanic looking blokes, pissed sitting on the bed. This was the first time I had had the confidence to potentially have to look after myself and it felt good...really good.

Now remember I am a short time after a stroke and still pretty sore chest wise so I wont tell you exactly the next few minutes but I can state categorically that the Puerto Rican Dance party ended right there and was never heard of again over the rest of my stay!! The threat of inserting their Boom Box rectally may have had a small contributing factor.

Anyway as you can imagine my adrenaline levels were totally off the scale so any chance of going back to sleep was gone. I decided to watch the dawn come up in the wonderful bar at the stern of the ship. The area had 24 hour coffee and croissants but more importantly had an entire wall made of glass which formed a wonderful viewing gallery onto the Mediterranean. I settled down and started to relax and think. As I stated earlier I believe whatever your religious persuasion when you have a life threatening illness you do deals with a God or higher spiritual being. So I am sitting there on my own and totally enjoying the whole experience and I think hang on I haven't seen any dolphins on my trip, which was now over a week old. I had even bought along binoculars to help me find these amazing creatures. So I said in my mind "If I see a dolphin today I am going to get better". I know many of you believe in the law of abundance and many will have read The Secret as I have, but what happened next will stay with me forever. Literally only 15 seconds passed and then two magnificent dolphins sprung out of the water, only perhaps 20 feet from the boat. They were in perfect unison and glistened like diamonds in the early morning sun. I cried and cried, as it was so beautiful and emotional. As they dove under the water I gave thanks to the entire universe for this most exquisite of gifts.

I never saw them again or for that matter any other fucking dolphins during the following nine days. However I had called and the universe had answered, Bob wasn't going to beat me …. God had spoken!

16th June 2015
Tone's travel tips
If you have a coughing fit and some big fat sweaty American tells you
Boy you'd better stop smoking .....retort quickly and clearly
"Oh I'm sorry I have cancer" will make them shut the fuck up very quickly
I enjoyed that much more than in reality I should have

19th June 2015
Yesterday I climbed Mount Vesuvius. The enormity of it was quite stupendous. In truth I took a little video when I reached the top and I was in literally floods of tears with the sheer relief of actually achieving something. It was unbelievably hot and at times I nearly gave up and turned around. But why did I do this?
I wondered why on earth did I feel compelled so much to get to the top
Was it bravado
Was it the fact that I knew it would engender loads of approval from my friends
Was it to test myself
All these maybe a little
The real compelling reason was that it made me feel normal and pre cancer again
And that's what made the trek the worthwhile journey
Just to feel normal after what is now eight months of being aware of something in my body that could kill me
Even with the one lung issue I felt whole again
Off to the blue Mosque in Istanbul
I have my Liam Neeson from Taken jacket and a somewhat lacking set of skills.

BREAKING BOB

21ˢᵗ June 2015
I want to share an intimacy but shhhhhhhh don't tell anyone
ok
I'm just sitting in the bar cogitating life again
I don't want to be morbid but I know I may not potentially be
out of the woods yet
So I was thinking are there any other loose ends I need to tie
up in the event of me not getting over this
One came to mind who would carry me in the old box thing
So which of my friends would do this
Men who I love respect and wouldn't drop me and feel likewise
about me
Also combinations like 5 big buggers and then say Graham
Wendes who is a bit short . I could see him in some form of
high heels to be able to keep up
Then I realised I'd narrowed my list down to 15
That's 15 men who I can genuinely call friends
All martial artists except for by old boss Daryl Clarke
But to have that many beautiful and amazing friends who I
know I could trust and rely on was an amazing feeling
I won't list you but you know who you are
So thank you for being in my life and thank you for making me
realise just how blessed I am

How bloody apt when we re-examine this later on when the funeral plans take shape.

23 June 2015 - Venice, Italy
It's my last night away
Then home for a couple of hours and then Glastonbury
I have had the most wonderful of times and I humbly thank
you lot for sharing my travels and a adventures with me
The places I have visited have been wonderful

126

But the people I have encountered have been the key to this
being an epic journey
Having that link to home, an anchor if you like. Has
empowered me enormously
I have done myself proud I think
And made some lifetime friends from a over the world
I was right to do this and I deserved it wholeheartedly
I feel enriched and defragged mentally
I'm certainly stronger and I believe be more able to deal with
the tribulations looming
I've had a fucking ball
Thanks for being part of it
Namaste xx

24th June 2015
This is interesting
My pulse at rest before the break was 106
This was mainly due to my heart having to work harder due to
only one lung
Now it's at 80 which I am really pleased to see that progression
I arrived back at some unearthly hour to be picked up from
Southend Airport by a Glasto mate Pronoy Bose who kindly
dropped me off home in Coventry....now off to Glastonbury for
the wonderous festival.

GLASTONFUCKINGBERRY
25th June 2015 · Pilton, United Kingdom
Shit I'm exhausted
Back at 1.30am last night up at 6am
Miles of walking with a heavy rucksack
I set myself a goal last December of getting here to Glastonbury
come hell or high water
I bloody made it although in truth I nearly bailed this morning

as I didn't feel that well
Off to bed now after watching Florence and the Machine
Night all

One of the two goals I set myself after the operation was to make sure I got to Glastonbury. I turned up at the bus park at some ungodly hour and met up with the mighty Ken, his daughter Kate and her boyfriend Sam. I had bought new camping equipment, including a tiny claustrophobic tent, all designed to cut the weight I had to carry to an absolute minimum. Even so it felt I was carrying the entire All Blacks front row on my shoulders. But it was great to be there and off we toddled to the wilds of Somerset. I usually camp at an area called Southpark two, a thirty minute walk from the gate we were dropped off at. Because of my weakness the travel time was well in excess of an hour and I truthfully only made it because my travelling partners took it in turns to help me carry my gear.

As it turned out this was probably my favourite festival EVER. I met The Antipoet, *who kindly gave their services for free at the Warriors Assemble Dinner later on that year. Ironically Paul Eccentric's Mum is now suffering from cancer and we are trying to get her to take a more holistic approach to her treatment. The highlights were numerous: The Who closing the event, Patti Smith in fine passionate fettle, Lionel Richie just being incredible, Burt Bacharach replaying 'rain drops keep falling on my head' when a small shower erupted which was legendary and getting to the front row of the Wilko Johnson gig. But the one incident which stands out was something that could only happen within the confines of the Glastonbury experience. I saw that the Dalai Lama was giving a blessing in the Stone Circle area.*

Mighty Ken and I walked the short distance from our tents and took our place in the field and listened to his Holiness for an hour in the pouring rain. It transpired that it was his 80th birthday. So, in the middle of a muddy field in Somerset, a few hundred hardy souls (many who obviously hadn't been to bed after a major Saturday night before) sang Happy Birthday dear Dalai or was it Lama? I can't remember. What an extraordinary man and what an extraordinary experience. He spoke of the power of engaging with life and of helping your fellow man; all of his words resonating deep inside me. This was worth the pain and the struggle of getting there on its own. Namaste, you beautiful creature.

I quote the wonderful Lisa Lynch of The C-Word *fame here and once again her and my stories intertwine. She also had the Glastonbury bug and had set the target of getting there after the Bullshit had been removed. We may even have met, or crossed paths, as I was there the year she went. I cannot tell you just how much I admire this woman and her amazing writing.*

The way she wrote about it:
"Getting to Glastonbury with P. Tills and Si (she says as though it can be equated to reaching the summit of Everest or Mandela's Long Walk to Freedom) wasn't just a big deal in terms of how far I have come in the space of my 'gap year" but in recognizing that it is possible to fall right back into the comforting arms of the stuff you love (or love listening to) like jumping off a perilous tightrope into a huge enveloping cushion. And the simple fact that it all happens on a farm in Somerset only adds to its brilliance. Because when you are low on signal, when text messages take 48 hours to reach you (its better now in all honesty) and when you are miles away from your laptop and your email and are so far removed from your communication crammed life that you couldn't do without at home. And strangely comforting as it is the rest of the time you are not continually having to return hospital questionnaires or order repeat prescriptions or book follow up appointments or answer questions several times a day about how are you. And by heck it is glorious."

29th June 2015
"Well, my friends, the time has come
To raise the roof and have some fun"
Well that's been the last three weeks of my life and I'm home again now. I bloody made it ....though in honesty a couple of times I didn't think I would. ~I nearly bailed on Glasto but

that's another story.

I bloody made it and am mighty pleased with my journey. Friday I'm back in the hospital to see if Bob has completely fucked off or not... bit scared but I'll deal with it. My reason for writing tonight is to offer my sincerest thanks to **Sarah, Andy Haynes Mike Knight Stephanie Woodward Rich Green** and the rest of the team for covering my absence of the past time whist I have been recuperating (or having a blast) for the past wee while and in reality the past 8 months. I'm hoping to be back badder, madder and more eccentric than ever.

I am so pleased I went in the dojo for two mins tonight ...what a wonderful heartfelt welcome. Thank you so much and to **Graham Wendes** who bought me back from Birmingham.... cheers matey.

2nd July 2015

I've been awake since 3-30am this morning. My latest bubble is coming to an end and I'm getting scared ....really fucking scared

I went to an open day at the Hospital yesterday and popped in to the Arden Cancer Centre to say hi to the radiographer team. I took them in a piece of pumice from my Vesuvius Adventure and got all the accolades I really went in there for. To show them how far I had come since my stroke and knowing everyone would say how well I look. And I do feel better and stronger the break not only gave me some much needed R and R and (a mental defrag).

This bubble has now lasted three months and has been a lovely respite from worry. This Friday I will know or at least start to know if the radiotherapy worked.

One of the girls in the team (my fave) came to say hello. She couldn't believe how well I'd done ESPECIALLY AFTER THE

MASSIVE DOSES of radiation I had and the amount of cancer that was left after the op. Ouch that hurt!!
I then had a little health check thing done at the event Cholesterol 4.0 5 star there Mr P. Blood Pressure spot on 5 star there Mr P. PH 8.30 OH I've just had a Lucozade so that's ok 5 star Mr P. Whoa woke up this morning last one fucking bad news. My blood PH is a breeding ground for cancer. Because I've taken my eye off the ball as I was too busy having fun and basking in the hundreds of messages from my trip. I have lost sight of what I was trying to achieve with my diet. I apologise for not being upbeat but I am so angry with myself. I don't want chemo yet I have flouted the very info that I have gleaned and just ignored it cos my ego took over and I like drinking a lot when on holiday

3rd July 2015
Here we go then
The next hour may very well define the rest of my life
No pressure there then
This was at 10 am
Great outcome so far scan needed but he very pleased with my progress
Gordon's alive
Scan booked to confirm his thoughts
I'm pleased thus far but the scan results are the real one
Not unhappy with this
Phew

3rd July 2015
Second hospital appointment a tour de force as well
Lung physio looks like next check-up will be my last
Good lung good

Bad lung no crackles
A good good day
Bloody marvellous

9th July 2015
It's my birthday on Saturday but tomorrow I am at the doctors
and then at the wonderful Kevin Mills and Jenni Mills British
Kenpo Union Summer Camp teaching alongside some fabulous
martial artists. What a great weekend looming in the company
of excellent friends round a campfire ...so I am writing this now
as I won't be contactable for the weekend.
I do like to pontificate on this day and went back to last year's
message (to be pasted below shortly) and thought just how
bloody prophetic my words were then Pillages Birthday
Message to the nation 2014
Greetings minions.
Well another year older but certainly little wiser. It has as
many of you know been a weird past 12 months. What have I
learned from it? First and foremost, the value of true
friendship. At my lowest ebb, people have come forward
unexpectedly and without a moment's thought for their own
feelings and stood by me offering that most precious of
gifts...unconditionally.
This year I have lost three friends, two to cancer. I have to say
it affected me more than I could have imagined. All younger
than me as well. That feeling of mortality is a horrible one
when it hits you bang in the middle of your very soul. Make the
very most of your life dear people...it is a precious gift that we
take far too lightly at times.
I have learnt this year to pick my battles more wisely and
perhaps be truer to the person I really am, that's been a major
part in my evolution and has made my life a lot less stressful.

I have realised that I do have a gift of reaching into people's hearts and helping them with their own struggles. I believe, as I get older, this will form a major part of my journey. I love the feeling of changing a life for the better. It's good to have a Pillage sized lunatic on your side I think.

I realise that I do l and will always carry this zest for existence throughout my life. Live with passion my friends otherwise what on earth is the point of just existing...shuffling meekly towards that mortal coil. Say fuck it and arrive out of breath, skidding to an abrupt halt and say what an amazing journey.

I have been privileged to have been able to live such a life thus far. I will do my utmost to continue that for very many years to come. I have taken the path less travelled at times...sometimes well often bad, but in truth there is very little I would have changed. I apologise genuinely and wholeheartedly to those I may have hurt on the way but I will not ever apologise for the person I am and will be.

Like bloody hell. I could just copy and paste those words and they would hold the same strength but for so many other reasons. Another year older and wiser.... well maybe. I have learnt that I am a million times tougher than I gave myself credit for.... I am also a million times weaker, but that's OK. This year many hundreds of new people have followed my journey and I am grateful to each and every one of you, because sincerely I would NEVER have coped with this last year. I have learnt that I am deeply loved and cared for far more than I deserve at times and I thank you for that as well. So once again unconditional love and friendship is my number one feeling. I have lost many friends this year ... mainly to Cancer. We have all lost someone I guess. I am drawn particularly to two gentlemen Ronnie Colwell Sensei who shared a birthday with me and the legendary Sifu Dave Carnell both who I never met but were remarkable martial artists and I know who are sorely missed.

I promise to do my very best to be here next year on my 55th !! Friendship comes in many forms but the real friends (and you know who you are) please pat yourself on the back for a job bloody well done over the past nine months especially. After the stroke/TIA's I am not as sharp as I was I think so if I forget things at least I have a valid excuse eh !!

The day after my operation, 2nd December I set myself the goal of getting to Glastonbury and I managed to do that with some poise as well as climbing Vesuvius...both highlights of a troubled year. So again my friends please realise the thing you haven't got is time.....so go and enjoy this most precious of commodities. Believe me when you have looked closely at your own mortality as I have take these words as gospel !!

My other highlights were the MAI Awards and the Martial Arts show. I could not even begin to tell you the warmth and love towards me there. More importantly so many people came up and thanked me for helping them or their family with addressing cancer. That makes what I have endured so far more bearable. We need to reach out far more people who are in trouble, I realise that as well. If the children really are our future we owe it to them to be far more vociferous and far more willing to fight for those things which ail our society so so much.

I once again and look back on my life and fuck me it's been fun and I wouldn't change much I promise you.

Namaste xxxx

Pillagius Maximus

11th July 2015

You know life is good when you get 70 people singing if anyone can the cancer man can on your birthday. What a fabulous birthday this was. Teaching on the same bill as Mo Teague and Kelee Arrowsmith (another cancer survivor and warrior) from South Africa and spending time with such amazing friends. I will never forget the infamous Lube Cake incident and the Hula Dance off with Mighty Mo Teague. I won btw...he see's it differently but we were both bloody magnificent to say the least.

17th July 2015

I'm off to the doctors today, well infact to the surgeon department to see how I am doing. The truth is I feel bloody great at the moment. Taught my wonderful adults this week and back on the mats teaching and a little training for the foreseeable future. Also back to the Gym on Monday. I am aware that this may only be temporary...Bob as we know is a stubborn fucker. However today it feels damn good to be alive and I will do my utmost to enjoy it
They are checking to see if the chest structure is compromised as I am still having mucho pain from one of the, still I believe, broken ribs that has set awkwardly
But I'm feeling GOOOOOOOOOOOOOOOD to paraphrase the mighty James Brown.

18th July 2015

Many thanks to everyone for their kind comments yesterday. The hospital visit yesterday of course was brilliant so that means I am no longer under the pulmonary team or the surgical team. The big one of course is getting the all clear from the Oncologist. This sadly is a long way off but I will deal with this when the time comes.
Looking forward to tonight meeting up with friends in Manchester for some boxing shenanigans........

27th July 2015
I had my thermal imaging scan today
Il get the results later this week
It looks as if there is still some Bob left
I was expecting it to be honest
Time to up the anti on the holistic diet front as I've decided
whatever I won't be doing chemo
All good though
Pillage is fighting fit and being awesome x

27th July 2015
Let me tell you a little about the WONDERFUL people who did
the scans. The company is called Medical Thermal Imaging
and is under the directorship of Phil and Rosa Hughes two
incredible people who I am honoured to now call friends. They
have literally imaged thousands of people over the last six
years as more and more women are waking up to the fact that
they have a choice of breast screening/imaging and don't have
to suffer exposure to ionising radiation and painful and
dangerous compression of the breast. Many men have also
benefited including of course myself.
Rosa and Phil were introduced to Digital Infrared Medical
Thermal Imaging in 2006 when Rosa discovered a large lump
in her left breast. She was only 42 years old and was advised to
have a mammogram and biopsy to diagnose the status of the
lump. Rosa had concerns about the safety of both the
mammogram and biopsy on the grounds that she didn't want
to increase the risk of cancer by exposure to ionising radiation,
or spread the cancer under compression, or even seeding from
the biopsy.
Discovering Thermography was the answer to their prayers,
no ionising radiation, no compression and it could rule out the

need for biopsy. Rosa's first thermal imaging showed that she had a 96% risk of malignancy (high risk) and that angiogenisis was detected. She embarked on a total lifestyle change and used thermal imaging to monitor her progress every three months until the scan showed her breast health had reduced to low risk.

Rosa and Phil were so delighted they decided to buy their own camera and share the good news with as many women as they could. Although it was breast imaging that had first alerted them to the benefits of thermography, Medical Thermal Imaging Ltd now offers far more than just a breast imaging service. Thermography is a physiological picture of the body and is suitable for all ages of men women & children. Based on a farm in Lydiate (see pic) near Liverpool, the company's mission is to offer a method of imaging for men, women & children of all ages. With regards to breast health Phil & Rosa are working towards a safe routine breast imaging program to include all women from age 20 onwards. They also have produced a multi award winning documentary which is called The Promise about their work. I cannot not tell you what unbelievable work they are doing. If you need any info their website is www.medscans.co.uk or telephone 0333 8003003

30th July 2015

Pillages fabulous news time

Just spoken to the Thermal imaging unit, and it looks as if things are going really well. There is nothing in their to indicate that things are going bad, got one little area which is around my chest which is a little bit concerning...but everything is looking fabulous, not to say I haven't still got cancer as I probably still have...but looks as though it might be under control and it's not spreading!!

3rd August 2015
I've read the wonderful words about today from Eddie Quinn, Mikey Wright, Andrew Holland and of course Paul Taylor and we had a doody. Gentlemen I cannot offer such mighty verbiage as thy good selves but I can say this, your exemplary company made me forget all day I have cancer. That's no mean feat so my humblest thanks for a day of happiness and wonder.xx
I am blessed to have you guys as my friends

4th August 2015
Well another milestone today I went back to the gym
I can't swim as my deflated lung won't allow it but I'll work on that
My weight was about a third of what it was before the op
The stair climber was farcical
As was the chest press
However I bloody did it
I need oxygen...lots of fucking oxygen...preferably laced with Pernod .

The swimming was actually far harder than I thought it would be. It took a whole year before I could even swim a single length of a 25m pool!

5th August 2015
WTF??? !!!!!!
I had a chat with my Oncologist last night. Bless him he was working at 8.30pm but still found the time to answer my concerns. I cancelled my CAT scan last week after reading it

was the equivalent of having 800 chest x - rays and wanted some info before doing it. Don't worry Mr. Pillage a normal person is exposed to five units a year in background radiation, if you worked at a nuclear power plant you are allowed to be exposed to fifty units per year. The scan will only expose you to ten units and when you consider I exposed you to 60,000 units during your treatment it really is nothing. FUCKING HELL No wonder I felt a tad poorly. Just ordered a Spiderman T shirt in case I develop superpowers .....well more superpowers to be honest !!

6th August 2015
Last January 28th I was given six months to live
That time in now up
Not only surviving but thriving
The cancer will probably get me but not today
Bob you little bastard knob off I've got hell of a life to live

12th August 2015
Medical help needed. For a long time after my op my heart rate resting was 108 ish. I am now about 95 even after starting to exercise over the past week. As I have only one lung and the other is apparently quite compromised by the radiotherapy (as is my heart) what sort of figure should I look at getting to and what would be the upper limits when exercising. I was told about 133...any help appreciated
I have to say for the past week I've been very breathless...going back to my breathing exercises
I can only manage five mins max on a stair stepper
My lung physio said I had to get fitter by doing a lot of sit ups from chairs, I find this hard as my knees are knackered at the moment. The stepper is the nearest I can get to that. I'm not on a mission to prove anything I just want to get to the bit where I go up my stairs and don't want to pass out with breathlessness

16th August 2015
Let me be clear I really really want BOB to do one now but I tell you the fear of dying makes you like your life sooo much better. It's a shame we don't realise that earlier

17th August 2015
One week down the line
Resting pulse down to 85
Oxygen saturation 95%
That's a week or trying rock salt inhalers some good training and breathing exercises
80 target pulse for next Monday
I'm happy with that given my one lunged status

17ᵗʰ August 2015
Interesting gym session. Managed nearly two mins, when an elderly Indian gentlemen came over and asked for a word . He has just been diagnosed with prostate cancer and was feeling scared. Apparently I am a bit of a celeb up the gym and they told him to come and speak to me. Left him in a much better place.

23ʳᵈ August 2015
TBH I woke up a bit wobbly today. I'm very concerned about this lump they've found join my neck which I had put down to just muscle pain. Awake at 5am fretting.
However, I looked at a picture this morning and it warmed my heart to realise that every one of the gentlemen in the pic and the others I have named I am privileged to call a friend. In fact there are 3 of my pall bearers (Village People) in it.
Feeling blessed

24ᵗʰ August 2015
I really don't need this got bad facial tingles, dizziness and a very sore carotid and Royce Gracie arriving later. Bit worried if honest...waiting for a call from the doctors. Wish me luck I'm actually quite nervous.

25ᵗʰ August 2015
If you had a day just one day of complete madness then yesterday had it all. From a scare with new tumour, blowguns, "blue smarties", a red whip, a shock knife, Royce Gracie and about a million laughs well that was my world on a rainy Monday night in Coventry. My deepest thanks to all the attendees...my dear friend Ross Hudson (Força Combat Academy) whom I realised last night that it is a very good thing that we live a reasonable distance apart or there would be

much Fuckerey spread .... eh Buttercup ? Great to meet Tom and of course as ever Royce Gracie on outstanding form both as an instructor and genuine human being. I cannot tell you how much I respect this man not only for his obvious achievements but how he conducts himself as a person. Wonderful wonderful friends sharing their world with others.

25th August 2015
Resting heart rate now down to 72 with oxygen saturation at 95%
That's the best since the op
Very pleased

26th August 2015
I'm tired I think it's the 48oz of veg and fruit I'm taking a day.........
I had two meetings with my nursing team today.... sadly both are saying I have a lot of red flag markers in my neck I should be concerned with. Roll on the scan next week to find out exactly what is going on...
If all good I may well throw a mahoosive party xx

28th August 2015
"So far, I have decided to take whatever my disease can throw at me, and to stay combative even while taking the measure of my inevitable decline. I repeat, this is no more than what a healthy person has to do in slower motion."

Managing Emotions and Coping - Christopher Hitchens Fellow Cancer Sufferer now sadly dead from January 2012 Vanity Fair

Hillz FM

During August I was asked to be a guest on an old students of mine radio show. Paul Sanders or Festipaul (his DJ name) does a morning show for Hillz FM a community radio station based in an area of Coventry called Hillfields (hence the name). Paul had reached the level of black belt and for a while had run classes on my behalf before finding a new art to persue ... acting. Paul concentrated his questions on how I was fighting the cancer, my martial arts and of course Glastonbury. I had a fabulous time and really liked the whole vibe of the place. The show went really well and I enquired about how he got to become a radio presenter, which was really straight forward. Anyhow, the station manager had listened to the show and was impressed with something about me. Within a week I had done an audition and within two had my own show Pillage The Spiritual Warrior was now a regular on the radio, how fucking cool was that.

A year later I am still on air (God knows how) and have a great slot at 9am on a Wednesday morning. During my ill times the mental break of putting together the show and the time in the studio was a fabulous distraction. I cannot state just how precious the time down there is to me. I know that it helped me inordinately and to spend time with such fabulous and creative people has changed me for the better. Ta Hillz and the Watch Charity who run the station.

1st September 2015

Don't like this morning. I've woken up with a severe unease. I suppose its cos my next scan is looming and I'm worried shitless about my neck. I haven't had this feeling for months. That horrible pit of despair in your stomach. I'm allowed a down day but god it's hard

3rd September 2015
Oh well today is scan day. I always get emotional and worried when these come round as you can imagine. Meeting with the oncologist has been moved forward to next week. I am naturally worried about the lump in my neck I'm also really pissed off that I will be missing my private lesson with Nasser Butt over in Leicester this afternoon learning some wonderful Tai Chi. What will be will have to be but I'm strong, ruggedly handsome and of course capable of beating most things I hope. Tata xx

3rd September 2015
Had the scan. Thanks SOOOOOO much for all the private messages and texts ...wow. I'll know the results next Thursday. Feeling strong and full of derring do which is far better than feeling full of herring Poo xx

7th September 2015
I cannot believe that it's a year next month that I was diagnosed with cancer. What a year, Jesus. Would not be here now if it wasn't for the care and love offered from my amazing friends. Cannot thank you lot enough Namaste you beautiful people xx
I've decided that I'm not gonna be the bloke who died after a "long battle with cancer" Instead it will read cancer died after a long battle with the ruggedly handsome Pillagius Maximus !!

9th September 2015
I'm sitting here with my first major cold since my operation thinking ...oh lordy. I'm obviously petrified of any type of chest infection so I'm getting myself ready for that possible battle. More importantly, I get the results of my last scans tomorrow. This is the BIG one for me. Nervous you bet ......the thing is the

rest of my life in many ways will be dictated by the findings the wonderful Dr Hocking will share. Aghhhhhhhhhhh

I must add a brief note about my oncologist Mark Hocking. Over the next two years I would have many meetings with him. He would ALWAYS return my messages, mostly at about 8pm at night. I even had a call on a Friday evening at some silly time. I guess his workload is that intense.

When I first met him I was struck by his calm and matter of fact demeanor and hard-working attitude. When Mr Marzouk, my surgeon, asked me which doctor I wanted for my treatment after the operation I turned it around and asked him who HE would choose. Dr. Hocking was his choice so that why I went with him. I am pleased beyond measure that this has been the case. If you read this then I cannot thank you enough for your patience and that fact you hardly ever rolled your eyes when I explained my next madcap idea for trying to keep me alive. Sir I salute thee with awesomeness.

10th September 2015

Off to the gym for an hour in a moment to stop me thinking too much about my meeting later. 12 o clock is looming. My gut feeling says it'll be OK.....but I am mentally prepared for the worst. Can't lose really !!!
Let's have a resounding WOOF
The outcome is as follows
The lump in my neck has been investigated
They don't know what it is but PROBABLY not a tumour
There is still cancer in my chest but has stayed about the same so no spread which is fabulous
I have quite a bit of pulmonary fibrosis in my good (oh how I laughed) lung but that probably won't get a lot worse hence

breathing issues
Back in three months
I asked him should I feel happy with the way things sit at the moment and he said yes... No change is good
I should feel happier I think but strangely subdued
So many thanks for all you lot for the love and support as ever
Namaste x

I've been cogitating. I know why I am not whooping. A lot of what he said was prefixed by the word PROBABLY. The Pulmonary Fibrosis PROBABLY won't get worse, the lump in your neck is PROBABLY not cancerous, and the cancer in your chest PROBABLY hasn't spread. Now I know what the problem is then. I PROBABLY will feel a bit better!

13th September 2015
Yesterday I met the Stephen Hawking of nutrition, the Einstein of Biological Science and possibly the leader of the Expendables!
Paul Coleman bought up a man called Jimmy from Hungary. The most knowledgeable person I have ever met...period. Gave me some great info to combat Bob. He will be coming up for a day at the dojo. I can't even begin to explain part of what he does in aligning your body's energies but JESUS H what a geezer. Thanks Paul ..... both Graham Wendes and Sarah Pillage took one of his tests to check all their organs for every. I WAS HEALTHIER!!!!!!!! I only had one lower mark for my respiratory system. The rest seems to be in good nick. I'll let you know when he is coming up and as your friend if you don't come then you are a twat...end of
Jimmy Ronin my deepest thanks and salutations. It was a genuine honour to share some time with you.

24th September 2015
Have arrived in the Isle of Man
Have come to this glorious Island to support my mate Scott Caldwell who is fighting in a white collar boxing event to raise money for a local hospice. I'm here with the legends that are Russell Jarmesty and Keith Priestly (and his lovely wife Sylve) what on earth could go wrong.

25th September 2015
Last night I met a lovely pair of ladies at Scott's weigh in
We ended up talking about Bob where one of the ladies said she had had a couple of scares with Cancer
We chatted about diets and what she could do about the future
She pm'ed on Facebook last night
"I'm glad I met you for your advice it gave me hope."
What a lovely thing to say
As this whole new life unfurls I know more and more that I have to become a voice to break down the taboos regarding cancer

27th September 2015
I'm so disappointed we never got to Zara Phythian and Vic's wedding last night as my breathing was terrible. I've seen some pics and it looked amazing. May you guys be blessed. Luckily I have an appointment with the respiratory team tomorrow. It's getting a lot worse again even though I am getting more active as much as I can.

28th September 2015
Oh great
Just finished with my specialist
I may have a heart problem as my pulse is all over the show

And the oxygen sats are fluctuating
Hey ho another journey
They want a full lung analysis as well
Marvelous !

29th September 2015
I was interested in the programme on tonight ... Body Donors
I could only watch it for a few minutes
All the fears and doubts came flooding back about my cancer
Not as tough as I reckoned then
I've never done particularly well with reality !!!
Also my bloody chest is as sore as hell tonight
Really sore
Still I have to remember I'm still alive and ruggedly handsome
!!

2nd October 2015
One year anniversary of being told I was ill
Never thought I would make a year

3rd October 2015
Yesterday was my anniversary of the news of getting cancer
Yesterday I nearly managed to swim a length of the pool
Nearly bloody killed me
Off to play squash now followed by three hours of teaching
Positive outlook means a positive life
Also too stubborn to give in
My ego wouldn't allow it

6th October 2015
Just got back from the Doctors
Looks like my heart was " collateral damage" from the
radiotherapy as is the pulmonary fibrosis in my lung which

will be a long term burn and get progressively worse
"Just do what you can for as long as you can" said the lovely
Doctor
So yet another chapter opens
Bring it on bitches
You ain't beat me yet
Time to book an spot with a cardiologist
Good news is I have a heart
Bit miffed but will keep smiling

Tone's Life Tips

Had an annoying, and I mean annoying, set of telephone cold callers today. Every single one of them opening with "How are you today?" says Brian of Virgin Media Slough (when in fact you know damn well his name is Gupta and he is in bloody Mumbai). My answer of "Not very good. I have cancer," really stops them in their tracks. Top tip...they usually hang up.

13th October 2015

Well I don't know why apart from maybe the new treatments i have been administering but I can actually breathe this morning. This is the FIRST TIME since last Dec. So thank you weird remedy......yeast, silica, liquorice root and some weird membrane stuff I salute thee...even if it's for a little while it's a yippitydo sort of morning...GORDONS ALIVE !! Let's have it you slaaaaaaaaaggggggggs, the dinners tomorrow.

Warriors Assemble

The First Supper

This was the ground breaking and truly fucking inspirational Award's Ceremony, Warriors Assemble, celebrating the very best of human nature and fighting spirit within the Martial Arts and it was started by yours truly.

The idea for the awards evening came to me after attending yet another atrocious Awards/Hall of Fame Dinner where people who have disabilities seemed to generally get ignored yet again, yet there are many, many thousands out there practicing their art to enormously high standards week in week out. As a now disabled martial artist, I thought it would be a wonderful idea to start a brand new concept, getting 10000000% away from the Hall of Fame debacles we have been plagued with over the past few years. I put out a request for nominations on Facebook and all of a sudden we had the making of an amazing evening, keeping the name Warriors Assemble as it central tenet.

We were inundated with incredible tales of people who have overcome huge obstacles and problems to further their love of their chosen discipline.

Over twenty-five awards were presented with over 300 people in attendance. There were one armed cage fighters, black belts with leukemia, one legged Judoka, kids with Aspergers, kickboxing teachers with cerebral palsy in wheelchairs, a blind karate sensei and so many more wonderful people who were just completely inspirational. There was at times hardly a dry eye in the house as one by one these martial artists shared their stories, maybe many for the first time to people who actually wanted to listen.

The evening ended and Kevin Mills stood up and asked for silence. On the big cinema screen a slide show started with pictures of me doing stuff from over the years. I was in stitches, then it really started. First came the video interludes. Graham Wendes talking about me, then Mikey Wright, Mike Knight doing his very best Rik Mayall impersonation, Gavin Richardson wearing a strange garb of a Darth Vader mask with a Viking biker helmet, (In truth I still have nightmares on this one). Steve Strong then galloped on screen with a pair of leather chaps and no discernable pants, Scott Mills and Notti narrating from their car and Danny Bigley as a construction worker. The last one was Tony Bailey who offered sage words about the sanctity of his friendship with me and like the others offered heartfelt words on just how much I meant to them. I honestly cannot even begin to tell you just how touched I was. He then looked directly at the camera and said Mr P there's no need to feel down I said young man (obviously the words to Village People's famous disco classic YMCA). I noticed a movement from the side of the stage and out bounded all of these fine fellows in full Village People garb with the song now blaring mightily through the rooms sound system. Literally three hundred people then stood up and started doing the strange dance that accompanies the song. I have never been so shocked. These magnificent bastards had given me my funeral whilst I was still alive and kicking and told me exactly what I meant to them whilst I was still here. No man ever felt more adored than me right then. As I may have mentioned elsewhere in the book, someone told me they didn't like this part of the evening as it seemed as if it were my epitaph. It was and I was one of the luckiest people on earth. Thank you again…I can say that ten minutes was one of the most

memorable highlights of a very full and wonderful life.
Namaste xxxxxxx

15th October 2015
Don't know why but I'm really struggling today with stuff going on in my head about everything....the cancer, fibrosis and dodgy ticker. Hate days like this...they don't happen often but when they do it makes you feel helpless and alone. I think this is my 10th bad one in a year so perhaps I am allowed but it's bloody horrible

15th October 2015
It's weird when I feel down and spill it on here it's like coughing up a fur ball and it usually helps loads
My problem is this bloody breathing
My oxygen sats are about 80 % and it's like breathing through a gas mask filled with treacle
It's so fucking scary at times
I missed a call from my doctor only to be told when I called back that I'd have to rebook
I need a pulmonary specialist at Brompton Hospital in London
Sorry for involving you lot but it does help loads

Thanks so much
Namaste x

20th October 2015
It's wonderful my breathing seems to be back again today.....

29th October 2015
Big day today
Off to Solihull for a first meeting with a Respiratory Specialist
Hopefully be able to get a handle on this fibrosis malarkey
Bit nervous but will be rickety boo
OK, I have had a good meeting with the specialist
Apparently the fibrosis scaring has destroyed 15% of my good lung but has probably stopped expanding now.
There is an area in the lung that didn't work that may be a problem but, fuck it, it's in the crap one.
All in all a good result
Onwards and bloody upwards my lovelies xx
I'm feeling good and more positive than ever
The reality is I am going to be working at about 40 % capacity of a normal person
But I ain't normal no fucking way xx

2nd November 2015
This is from the article below...please read it it's amazing
From a wonderful teenage girl whose name I will keep secret
"From the time these photographs were created until 2012 I was cancer-free. One month after I celebrated my fifth anniversary from the diagnosis, in June 2012, I became ill again. For months the doctors were uncertain how to label the new diagnosis. After a misdiagnosis and unnecessary chemotherapy, they determined it wasn't a new cancer, but

that the breast cancer had returned. It had spread to my lungs and brain.

Since then more chemo, monthly medication, chest and brain radiation, and Cyberknife have become a part of my recent experience, but only a fraction of the entire experience. According to statistics I shouldn't be alive right now, but I am. I've gained more from this experience than I've lost. I'm grateful for every moment of it."

8th November 2015

I have odd and quite intense pain coming on this week......time to go back to the docs just to be safe I think. All in new areas away from the original site.....poooooooooh

9th November 2015 ·

Been to the docs they are checking for blood clots in my lung....fucking whoop

That's why maybe I've been getting pains recently.....they are also scanning my gallbladder and liver.

What next Beri Beri, Ebola and sodding leprosy perchance !!

10th November 2015

Just had a call from the doctors

They want me back in ASAP for further tests

Poop

10th November 2015

The docs are doing tests to see if I've got blood clots in the lung

Will know for certain later tonight

11th November 2015

The doc phoned last night after the second lot of blood tests

seems to show no Pulmonary Embolism. This is more worrying if I am honest as the reality is that something is happening in my lung or gall bladder / liver. My biggest fear as I'm sure you can imagine is that BOB has gone walkabout. If so with all I have tried to accomplish over the past year has been in vain and I will be mightily pissed off. Onwards and upwards let's get this fucking battle won

11th November 2015

They are taking me in for scans at 3.30pm today
Gulp
#poopingoneself

11th November 2015

I have some news from the docs
I just got back from the doctors and as you can see I am happy and smiley. I have to share with you, with the ultra sound, I have an inflamed gall bladder, and because I have a collapsed lung, my gall bladder and my liver now sit under my armpit, now I know what it is I can deal with the pain……so basically I am a monster! Punch me in the Liver I bloody dare you hahahaha

A November Tale

A brief story from November, the dates are immaterial. I was shocked, as was most of the world to see the awful attack on the Bataclan in Paris where so many innocents died as a result of the terrorist attacks. As many people in my profession did, we discussed the various options one would face if such a horrific thing happened with you actually there. On about day three after the event, some one put up a pic on a thread on Facebook of the inside of the building showing the dead bodies. It was a horrific sight and I made a comment regarding

it. A moment later an internet troll flashed up "wish you had been there".

Remember I was still in a pretty dark place with my own mortality. I initially ignored it, not knowing the person involved at all, but gradually over the next couple of hours this man's comment started to annoy and needle me tremendously. In truth I got really pissed off and started thinking about how people get away with this sort of shit on the internet with no consequence of their actions and how upsetting this could be to people with a less robust mindset. I tried to befriend this man so he would read a very personal message I had written him, but to no avail. I put up his details on my wall to see if anyone knew him as his profile showed he lived in Coventry and within a few minutes not only I had him identified but his address as well....which was roughly a two minute car drive from my house. Oh deep bloody joy.

I hatched a cunning plan, which involved me paying a visit to his house. I went round there and literally parked the Hummer on his drive. I knocked brusquely on his door but no-one was in.

However, I noticed his next door neighbor looking nervously over the hedge. I strolled over and said do you know when "Mr X is back home ? I am an old friend and wanted to catch up. Please tell him that Tony Pillage called round !!". He said about 5pm and would pass on the message immediately he returned and looked somewhat relieved that I hadn't eaten him.

The following morning I popped round again but this time I was accompanied by Paul "The Titan" Taylor who had unexpectedly popped round for a coffee and a chinwag. For those of you who don't know Paul, he was at the time the UCMMA Heavy weight British Cage Fighting Champion and is a massive scary looking man. We popped round and caught the neighbor's attention again and said we were sorry to miss him but would be back later. I in the meantime had posted a copy of Martial Arts Illustrated with me on the front cover through the postbox with a politely, yet ambiguously worded letter asking why this total stranger had wished that I was dead.

At 5.01pm my phone rang and it was Mr X apologizing and promising he would never do it again. He had proverbially and maybe even physically shat himself from the sound of his voice. His niece had also contacted me in the afternoon saying that the guy drank and made an arse of himself on social media late at night and was a complete nuisance and had upset many many people. I spoke calmly and rationally but warned him about what he had nearly dropped himself into. I always harp on about people need to realize the consequence of their actions. He had learned a very powerful lesson that day. I still check his posts from time to time. He has calmed down a tad since then.

Pillage 1 Knobhead Keyboard Warrior 0

Cancerversary

1st December 2015
It's my Cancerversary. One year ago today at this very time I was being pushed down to the surgery that was to save my life.... where the hell has that year gone?

Happy fucking birthday
A year ago today I had an operation to get rid of BOB.

I remember lying on the gurney waiting to go into theatre and I did a little deal with the universe, I don't actually believe in God which makes this I suppose a bit ironic, I would happily have taken another year alive at that point, that was a year today and what a year it's been. The moment your told you have cancer, you think you're going to die immediately, the worst moment of my life, but I have to say in all honesty, this year has been one of the best years of my life because I have learnt to live. It's like a re-birth. I looked at the photograph from that year and that was me the day after the operation, if anyone wants to know the story behind that – ask Richard Barnes about me trying to savage the man in the next bed to me for being rude to a nurse, and there was about forty pipes coming out of me – I knew then, that I was going to stay alive, because I am that sort of belligerent bastard.

Today I am going to spend the day up in London, I am going to actually have a couple of hours for myself, I am going to go to the British Museum and have a look at some Medieval manuscripts... why? because I bloody well want to – then tonight I am going to meet some people who I know are going to be lifelong friends and hopefully travel back later – pissed on the train.

All you guys again, thank you, thank you for being there for me, nudging me, keeping me amused, and keeping me sane, God Bless you all xx

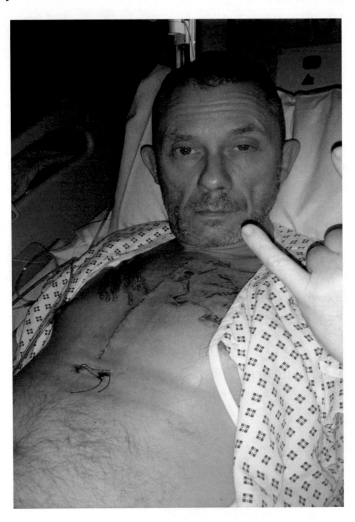

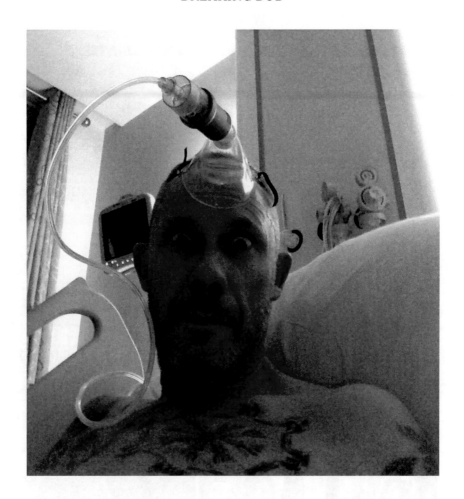

2nd December 2015
I am today having a consultation with the Breakspear Clinic in Hemel Hempstead for both my cancer and nutritional needs.

I had heard amazing things about this place from my friend Steve Rowe. Breakspear Medical has treated over 25,000 patients since 1982.

Starting as a family business over thirty years ago, it has earned global recognition for its contribution to the field of environmental medicine.

They have over fifty dedicated staff members including fully qualified doctors, nurses, accountants, laboratory technicians, nutritional therapists and administrative staff. I had booked a consultation with the head of the clinic Dr. Jean Monroe and her top nutritionist Ron Leon. Both were totally amazing and fabulous. They suggested I had some tests done, one where over fifty substances were introduced to cultures grown of my cancer to see what would affect it adversely, slow it down or kill it. Strangely much of my diet/supplements were spot on (i.e. wormwood, artemesian, B17 and K2). Thalidomide also seemed strangely to have a negative effect on BOB. Over the next few months I would be travelling down on a weekly basis for treatment (mainly Vitamin C injections) and thermal baths. The staff were excellent and treated all the clients wonderfully. However, the clinic is probably the world's leading centre for the treatment of Lyme disease. This tick borne illness made my cancer seem trivial and almost paltry if I am honest. It's an insidious bastard of a thing to go through and when I was having my Vitamin drip I would sit in the treatment area for up to six hours chatting to the Lyme patients and listening to their stories. Just be bloody careful people in areas where there are ticks in abundance...I would not want to go through that in any way, shape or form. Graham Wendes is now under their care and seems to be doing amazingly well with his oesephegal cancer. I could not recommend this place any higher.

6th December 2015
The end of another hectic week. The great news for me was I did a number of tests yesterday on my organ function (no

titters please) and have the vitality of a 39 year old... bloody whoop.

This pleased me immensely.

10th December 2015

Next meeting with the oncologist tomorrow
Don't want to tempt fate but I'm going to this one for the first time not petrified
I feel strong
Positive
And ruggedly handsome, but that goes without saying.

11th December 2015

Give me a resounding WOOF
All great at oncologists
Hasn't spread
All wonderful
Could not be happier
No appt for six months
If anyone can
The cancer man can
Xxxx

12th December 2015

Guys not to put damper on the great news from yesterday.....please remember I still have Bob, he just hasn't gone walkabout yet. The little tinker will probably get me but hopefully not in the foreseeable future. Thanks for all the fab messages though.... I'll say it now and say it again. I would not be here today I am convinced had you beautiful crazy lot been there with me on the journey. Your strength and love has enabled me to fight the battle of my life thus far. YOU are to be commended not I. Have a bloody wonderful weekend my loverrrrrrrrrrs !!

21st December 2015

I had an ultrasound last week and they found something on my lung
The thermal imaging scan I had today seems to confirm this
Bollocks Bollocks fucking Bollocks
Another battle to win
I'm stronger now and more belligerent
Bring it on son of Bob
Your Dad was found wanting
Thunderclunge xx

This was eventually found to be a burn from the radiotherapy on the pleural sac of my lung. Another scare for sure.

24th December 2015

I have literally just come off the phone to my thermal imaging doc
The latest scans show that the cancer has FUCKING RECEDED since the last scan in July
MERRY BLOODY XMAS TO ALL and especially me

31st December 2015

I look back to this time last year and could not have even vaguely predicted the mayhem that 2014/2015 bought into my life. Some of it was self-made, some probably as a result of my actions over the years and some just the way the cards are dealt to you.
I go into the New Year on the mend still and boy oh boy glad to be alive. At many times I honestly didn't believe I would make it through. However it's been a marvellous year in so many

ways. I have climbed mountains physically, spiritually and metaphorically and will continue to be the argumentative bombastic git that ever I am I hope !!

However, as I look back as I do at this time every year I do not focus on this strangely but the overwhelming feeling I get from 2015 is the value and sanctity of friendship and the unconditional love that this engenders. I am still overwhelmed by the outpouring of support I have had over the past year from so many people around the world, I promise you I would be in a far worse state had it not been for this. I thank each and every one of you for every message bon mot call whatever....

I won't mention too many people, as the list would take me until 12 tonight to write my thanks to you all. However there are a few friends I really must mention. If I have missed you out then its only because my fingers would have been bleeding by the end of all the typing and seriously I could have mentioned hundreds of you

Mike Knight and Stephanie Woodward plus Andy Haynes and Rich Green have all stepped up and magnificently to run the club when I wasn't up to it

Eddie Quinn, Richard Barnes and Mikey Wright your constant phone calls visits and texts have been magnificent thank you

Gav Richardson the mighty walloper...I hope your year gives you all you deserve

Maurice Teague and Andy Gibney my huge thanks to you chaps........

Steve Rowe with your shit going on yourself you have always had the time to chat and offer sage council

John Hammill and Paul Taylor but John especially thank you for your love and concern ... we are that brothers from another mother thing going on here

Nathan Hendry you know why....enough said you stalking

bastard.

Tony Bailey truly one of my highlights of my martial arts career has been crossing wands with you sir. People say I'm inspirational .....well if I am its only because I have spent time with people such as you my friend and Ric Lovett a new chap in the mix this year. I have a feeling that you and I will spend many hours in deep thought.

Ian Goehler who has visited from Manchester near enough every month since the diagnosis and phoned every day or texted. I cannot thank you enough my ginger love god.

The oddest one goes to Scott Caldwell. We didn't exactly start well now did we ...... however you and Russell Jarmesty are two friendship both of the greatest renown. I enjoy your honesty and directness. I have learnt much from both of you...my deepest thanks and respect

Daryl Clarke and Sarah Clarke always a pleasure. Daryl was the man who first believed in me as a person , I will always thank him for that

Graham Wendes and Steve Strong two members of the Pillage People ...the undoubted highlight of my year..... it ticked every box chaps

Carl Cooper and Neil Kirkland you pair of magnificent bastards. Warriors Assemble was an amazing event thanks to you two.

Karen Krankies McKay I love our weird friendship...thank you for being you ..namaste x

Paul Coleman a brother warrior......as is the redoubtable and also the irascible Mick Tully who I am pleased still likes me....just !!

Last but not least are the following Kevin Mills Leah-Marie Mills Jenni Mills clan of wonderments..your friendship has been amazing and thank you for your adoption of me.

However in a league of her own in the truly magnificent Sarah Pillage who has shown the true spirit of goodness and looked after me superbly and had it not been for her support I shudder to think where I would be right now. She didn't think I would make it through this year...as ever I like to prove you wrong !!! big big love Thank you Hutchy from the bottom of my heart

What advice can I offer to anyone of any note......DONT SMOKE might be a good one and 14 brave souls have promised me they are giving up . Well done.

More importantly though is this. Live in the moment and enjoy every last second of that experience. Don't procrastinate and have those experiences you crave NOW as the reality is if you don't the chance is you never will.

May 2016 bring you all peace , happiness and whatever floats your boat. Live your life to the absolute max and be as kind to people as they deserve. If not FUCK THEM UP BIG STYLE

What have I learnt?

I have learnt a lot this year, and achieved a lot, and I mean really have achieved a lot. Probably the highlight in many respects was the Warrior Assemble, which for many people it was the best Martial Arts events ever and that was down to us, I wanted to put something back, not just wanting to take.

Ironically - I have lost a lung, my heart is a bit shagged, I got fibrosis in the other lung, and to be honest, I have probably rarely been happier, it's about being in that moment, and being alive in that moment, not where I was at yesterday and it's not about tomorrow – its certainly hard when you have got oncologists meetings coming up and whatever else but to just live in the now is the most precious of gifts.

I shall be here next year have no fear.....
Namaste Mo Fo's xxx

4th January 2016

Back to the dojo today after a fortnight off. I had planned to do a lot of work on my book but have been sadly let down so will be cracking on it over the next few weeks.

Cardiologist on Wednesday to see what is wrong with my heart (yes I have one) don't faint

11th January 2016

I was reminded this morning by the news of Bowie's death from cancer just how lucky I am to be here. The operation had a 1 in 8 chance of killing me, the fact they found it before it was too late to operate was fortunate. The fact I didn't have a laser guided biopsy because Warwick Hospital screwed up several times meant that what was there didn't spread around my body. Guys please remember to live your life and not exist.......please I beg you

Sometimes we need this level of shake up to make us realise just how lucky we are to be here. Carpe the fucking Diem out of life me hearties.

You see the trouble is this. Once you've had that initial shite diagnosis no one will ever say the words "you are cancer free" again. No one. EVER. So to the medical professionals the word remission is the way forward, not letting them get into a whole pile of manure should the cancer come back, which sadly in many, many cases it bloody does. So there will be a lifetime of change, supplements, potions, pills, appointments, scans and worry. It's part of the process. But this year SOOO many wonderful people are going to die in the following few months. Lemmy of Motorhead, Alan Rickman, Caroline Aherne, Victoria

Wood, and Natalie Cole ...the list seems endless. All of them would have gone through the same set of feelings and emotions as the rest of us mere mortals when diagnosed. Bless you lot.

27th January 2016
My apologies this morning for my exit from the radio show
Felt lousy thought I was going to pass out
Back home
Can't think I will be back into work this week

29th January 2016
I had some test results back today
It would appear that the drug thalidomide seemed to kill my cancer cells
How weird
Looking into this with a lot of excitement
I knew I still have cancer but one little piece of me thought maybe just maybe they would say it had gone
But I will fight this in every way for as long as I have a breath in my body

The Thalidomide angle is a very interesting one. As I am sure many of you remember the terrible birth defects caused by this so called "wonder drug". Many women used it as an anti-morning sickness protocol. Unfortunately there were two versions. One caused the body to stop sending signals to create new blood supply connections. This is why so many poor children were born with stunted limbs. The principle works in the same way as a cancer treatment. The drug stops the tumour from getting blood supplied to it; therefore it cannot grow and will eventually wither and die. Well, that's the plan anyway.

11th February 2016

Off to The Breakspear clinic for the sit down on my blood cultures.....looooong day ahead

A very long day at the clinicians and another £2500 spent YIKEs.

I have had £188 of Vitamin C injected plus 3000000 units of D3. They are putting me on Thalidomide and doing a full detox. Head swimming a bit but I believe this gives me the best fighting chance to live

BRING IT ON CANCER BITCHES

After a lot of thought I decided that it would be best not to go the Thalidomide route as it may have some future connotations on my lung.

16th February 2016

Not long been back from the Docs. He thinks I have an internal bleed which is causing the pain and tiredness. Tests next week...bloody hell what next a phantom pregnancy.

17th February 2016

Interesting morning in hospital. Had heart scans which may show a faulty chamber and have been wired up for 48 hours on a heart machine. Tomorrow down to having 4 hours of infusions in Hemel then Friday Oncologist. Whoop aren't I the social butterfly?

18th February 2016

Another long day.......tomorrow they have moved my oncology appt forward two months. In loads of pain...lung, liver and torso. Really bloody nervous as I haven't had this much agony for 10 months. I foolishly thought it would be plain sailing but may be wrong.

19th February 2016
Just finished with the oncologist
Where the pains are is where Bob would naturally spread to
Sending me off for scans
Bricking it

19th February 2016
Looks like another battle ahead
Bollocks
I will win though cos I'm a stubborn twat

2nd March 2016
A message re Cancer funding
Amanda Wilding and everyone
Please help
I have had a very good gesture come from my very good friend
Amanda Wilding, she will be cutting her hair off to help raise
money to go towards my treatments, which is getting
ridiculously expensive. At the moment I am spending
somewhere in the region of £600 per week on treatments
down at the clinic plus a whole load of supplements, if you
could please help with this it would be fantastic and any extra
money made will be used on other people. I am in a very
fortunate position as I can kind of afford it, but its digging
down into all my resources financially. There are so many
people at the moment that cannot afford it, they just rely on
the normal medical processes, to be honest an awful lot of
them are not doing very well.
If you can help Amanda and myself, it would be brilliant, thank
you.

3rd March 2016
Down in Hemel Hempstead for another 6 hours of infusions and potions

9th March 2016
An odd day. Did radio show, then 2 hours teaching disengaged kids, followed by a private lesson then off to the Bablake School and back to the dojo. I also had the result of some scans which are not that great in many ways. One of the chambers in my heart isn't working properly which is compounding my breathing problems a tad. Bob may be visiting another area as well...little shit!. Yet I am still going on....I am though getting more and more fucking annoyed at people who sit around all day with the "problems" not working and sponging off the society. Man up and grow a pair you twonks

17 March 2016
Am at the clinic when one of the nurses came over and said ' you spread a little bit of magic when you are here which stays around for ages after you leave' and gave me a hug
Most happy xx

22nd March 2016
No wonder I feel faint my oxygen sats are down to 84%
 Its gonna be a long and horrible day
It's days like today that I remember how ill I am
I fucking hate it

30th March 2016
Just finished at hospital

2ⁿᵈ April 2016

For the first time since my diagnosis I feel so very angry at
what this fucking disease has robbed from me
It's far more than I ever realized both physically, mentally and
to be brutally truthful the path I had been on has been
destroyed. Fuck You Fuck You Fuck You

4ᵗʰ April 2016

Get the results of my last scan on Friday
Aghhhhhhhh shittinggoldones.com
Spending the day with my mate Graham Wendes who is having
a stent fitted.
I got a phone call today from my dear friend Graham. He
ironically is the one that first exposed me to the work of Philip
Day and the Credence Organisation. We had spoken a few
months previously at the rugby about his concerns about
swallowing food. It was either a hiatus hernia he thought or
cancer. Graham had been through the mill with family history
of it and with a diet that can only be termed FUCKING BIZARRE
he had for many years relied on vitamins and supplements to
help him. It turns out he has Esophageal cancer

7ᵗʰ April 2016

An interesting morning thus far
Went to the wrong hospital for my lung tests
Managed to get to the right one only five min's late
It appears that my lungs are working at only 36% of what they
should be
No wonder I'm out of breath
Bum !
Big day on the morrow
Get the results of the scans to see if Bob has spread
After a brief chat today with my Oncologist I am cautiously

optimistic
Whatever though I am prepared and ready to kick ass

Bob's Bobbed Off

8ᵗʰ April 2016
News about Bob
So I have just come out of the hospital, and I have got some great news!! They can't find any cancer!!
Now that's not to say it's not in my system still, but there are no tumours anywhere that can be easily identifiable.
So for the moment at least...BOB has FUCKED OFF.... and I could not be happier!
So I just wanted to say thank you everybody from the bottom of my heart.
I'm not saying for one second that he won't come back but for now we have beaten the little fucker, and it's down to me, a load of supplements, a load of oil and most importantly all the love and support you have provided me over the last few months, I love you all.

11ᵗʰ April 2016
What wonderful irony that the Pillage Party in Leicester yesterday coincided with the news on Friday that I have at least for the time being got the all clear for cancer. I cannot thank everyone enough for the warm welcome and love shown from EVERYONE who attended. My thanks of course as well to the wonderful instructors who gave up their time to be a part of this. Most of all thank you to **Danny Bigley**, whose effervescent energy and drive put it all together. Legend mate
Namaste xx

14th April 2016
What a difference a year makes in one's life:

15th April 2016

This has been an interesting week. I still can't get my head round I am tumour free. I know this may only be temporary but still it's a hard one to get around. Tonight I am going out with a group of my closest friends, a filmmaker, a Marvel Star and a Hollywood Martial Arts legend. Tomorrow hosting the British Martial Arts Awards at the national sports centre in Lilleshall. Tuesday getting a major award personally for my work in Coventry with helping kids.

Life is good

However, I would swap all these wonderful events for what happened on Wednesday. I taught two classes to kids of roughly the same age about seventeen. One group are kids who have completely disengaged from school the other at a private school ... so you couldn't get more different. Both sets asked how I was. I naturally told them about the positive news. Both groups were so happy it was unreal. Tears, whoops, high fives and hugs all round. That was worth more to me than any thing I could get at a ceremony. Thank you guys you made me incredibly proud. Namaste x

16th April 2016

British Martial Arts Awards 2016

What did well over 250 people have in common the weekend of 16th April 2016?

Yes, it was their attendance at the outstanding British Martial Arts Awards 2016 at Lilleshall National Sports Centre and believe me when I say "what an evening!"

The weekend... Almost stuck for words due to the exhaustion of the emotional experience so I'll have to borrow some expressions from someone very erudite who knows better than most about expressing these things, and who taught me "when you choose to look for the great in people, it tends to become apparent."

My usual profane superlatives have no place here. It was overall simply fabulous. The whole sense of humour, unbelievable energy and community throughout was like healing balm. The mutual respect from all those martial artists gathered under one roof was like being prodded with an arrow with a velvet tip. Special people, every single one of the hundreds who attended. The British Martial Arts Awards was one of those extraordinarily rare events where every time you turn around, or pass someone, or go to the bar, or for a wee, you start a whole new conversation with someone new that happily trundles wherever it wants. It was exciting to just chat to new friends with 'cheerful outlooks'.

The instructors and students from all angles, arms and aspects of martial arts - who can really cut the mustard - teachers with NO ego at all, but with a sense of humour that in no way detracted from their mission to share a wonderful evening, all chatting like old friends and brothers-in-arms and actively looking for common ground through which to engage and affiliate, transcended all the years of ego and politics, and buried the strutting uber-dans and money hungry leeches up their own arse.

It made a move away from the traditional Hall of Fame format where you buy a ticket ...you get an award. Every one of the 30 awards given was nominated by the public and then put to a panel of experts. Thereby meaning every single winner was fully deserved. In some cases people could not attend but were happily awarded their trophy and title as they bloody deserved it.

As my word-mentor for this post would say, "the whole weekend was fabulously exciting and invigorating, because everyone came together in the spirit of sharing and harmony, and whilst maintaining their own personal outlooks, yet remaining congruent with their own philosophies of trying to rise above the mundane, showed the best of themselves and enriched the whole experience for everyone."

In my own words, I think it was the best awards dinner EVER; this year, the strutting popinjays, egotistical idiots and bullshitting charlatans stayed away, because nowadays people don't suck up to them and are prepared to tell them to their smug faces...enough is enough. Let's get together in one place to really understand the spirit of martial arts. That place was the British Martial Arts Awards 2016.

From star of the next huge Marvel Film The British Martial Art Awards is exactly what the industry needs! Congratulations to the organisers for a fantastic event' Zara Phythian Marks - actress/martial artist star of the new Marvel Film Dr Strange. What can we say about the event? Well, I can only give you what I saw and the feedback from people both instructors and general public alike. I also sat down on the Monday morning and posted on Facebook partly as an aide memoire but also to try to get across the spirit of the evening. I sat for an hour writing about the little vignettes stored in my mind and I could have easily spent another and maybe another putting my thoughts to paper, it really was that good. But for nearly a week social media was awash with pictures, memories and wondrous stories.

My own highlights were Jacob Phelps, a young man with Downs Syndrome getting a standing ovation in the enabled Martial Artist of the Year Category as well as Brian Jones and Trevor Roberts Lifetime Achievement Awards. Brian has been training in the arts for over 70 years. What wonderful, wonderful men.

I had won the Martial Arts Man of the Year Award (sort of like Best Actor Oscar) by quite a heavy margin. When the award was presented the entire room to man stood up and gave me a standing ovation. I could not have been happier or more proud of the person I had become.

"I have been involved in martial arts events for over 30 years…this is the best event I have ever attended "
Don the Dragon Wilson, Hollywood Film Star and 11 times World Kickboxing Champion

Pride of Coventry Awards Night

24th April 2016

The end of my glorious few weeks
Cancer beaten (at least for the time being)
Martial Arts Man of the Year last Saturday
Coventry Community Champion
Meeting my hero Wilko Johnson
Now tonight been awarded my 5th Dan by my other
hero Trevor Roberts
I didn't think life could get any better but it just has
There is only one other person I would ever accept a grading
from apart from Mr. Roberts and he wouldn't ever have given it to
me.

The Funeral

During the whole course of the battle one aspect never ever sat right with me and that was the small matter of what the fuck to do with my funeral. The thought of being cremated in some soulless municipal crematorium or slowly decomposing in a box didn't really sit that well with me. I came up with all sorts of Pillage-sized madcap ideas...maybe stuffed and mounted in the dojo acting as a handy coat rack or even going to the Himalayas and freezing to death up Everest. The one that did sort of resonate though, was travelling to Nepal nearer to the end times as I had heard of a hospice there where you can be burnt on the banks of the Ganges, your spirit released into the mountains.

I liked this idea UNTIL the magnificent ginger love God Ian G recommended a film called 'What we did on our holidays,' starring the wonderful Billy Connolly. I had met the Big Yin several times in the past when he came to my hometown of

Brightlingsea to visit his cousin John. He was just as funny and perceptive as his stage persona and was probably my first ever man crush. Sad to think he now is also a fellow big C sufferer. The idea of the film is actually quite dark, but, I thought extremely funny.

A disjointed family travel to Scotland to see their father/grandfather who is dying of cancer. He dotes on his grandkids and takes them off to the beach for a heart to heart talk before he dies and to get away from the bickering family left in the house fulminating over the inheritance that is going to be fought over when he passes. In the middle of the chat he dies sitting in his favorite deckchair. He had been telling the children that he had just found out his DNA was of Viking stock (like mine). So they basically think to save all the arguing that would have gone on with his funeral arrangements, they make a raft out of driftwood, use the deckchair as a sail and cover the body with petrol from the car and light him up. Off he goes out to sea in full Viking mode. This was all set within the most beautiful remote Scottish coastal scenery.

This was it ...this was the bloody answer.

I phoned up a number of close friends and asked would they be prepared to do this. To a man all agreed. The plan then took off with some gusto. In my rugby days the Village People song Go West had figured very prominently during the formative years. The rule had been set...that song came on; all your clothes came off. I remember a particular incident in a kebab shop in Ipswich where the noble sport of Naked Sumo Wrestling was born. What a song to be sent off to, how apt!

Then I found out that people were actually arguing as to who would be the coffin bearers. My friend Scott Caldwell offered to do the setting alight by flaming arrow, Gav 'The Walloper' Richardson was going to greet people onto the beach dressed as the Grim Reaper. The actual Pall Bearers were to be as follows. Eddie Quinn (Construction Worker), Nathan Hendry (Hairdresser), Mo Teague, Mikey Wright (Biker), Steve Strong (Cowboy), Ian Goehler, Tony Bailey (Biker Policeman), Mick Tully, Richard Barnes as the Pastor and Mike Knight (Army) all dressed as members of the Village People. What a body of men to send you on the journey to Valhalla. These glorious bastards, this happy few, this band of brothers, true men one and all and the very best friends any man could ask for. Graham Wendes (now ironically also a fellow big C battler) was going to lead the procession in a tutu. His job was also to iron out the legalities of the plan.

Please note this is in no way a joke, it is written in my last will and testament. This wondrous idea really caught people's imagination and I, at long last, felt comforted that I was going to have the sendoff to end all sendoffs. I refer back to the comment by my old student, Connor Lake. I need to see you born aloft on shields when you die.....you are a warrior. This my friend's was going to be a proper Viking experience make no mistake and one to go down the annals of fucking history.

Wilko

The book has to end with this tale, full circle from introducing Bob with a Flashheart Woof to this. I always wondered when and at what point this tale should end. The perfect ending was presented to me on a Friday evening in, of all places, Leamington bloody Spa.

My all-time hero Wilko Johnson (legendary musician from Dr Feelgood *and* the Blockheads *with Ian Dury, but also renowned cancer survivor) was playing at the Assembly Rooms.*

I have been a huge fan of Wilko's music since my early twenties, having seen him play many times when I was living on Canvey Island. I loved the whole Feelgood *shit kicking pub blues and was also a fan of* Ian Drury and the Blockheads, *the other major band Wilko played in. But of course his amazing battle against cancer was what really set him on a pedestal for me. In my darkest days I used his journey to give me strength and insight.*

I called the mighty Ken to see if he fancied a road trip. By the time I had got through on the phone the gig had been sold out. Bloody bollocks. I checked StubHub and all the various outlets but to no avail. I called Mighty Ken and told him we were going to get in somehow. We did. I won't tell you how, but we did.

The gig, as one would suspect, was awesome. Wilko and his unique choppy guitar playing was ably accompanied by the effusive and incredibly sweaty Norman Watt-Roy on bass. About two thirds through the set my breathing decided to give up the ghost and I went to the back of the auditorium for some air. In the corner of the bar was a man selling t shirts and more importantly the new Wilko biography which I had been eagerly waiting to purchase. It was relatively quiet and I asked the merchandising guy (Mike) if he worked for the assembly rooms or was part of Wilko's entourage. As it transpired he was his best mate. I asked him did he have an address or PO Box number I could send my letter, from the previous November, to, to ensure the great man got it. This is the letter.

"Greetings Sir Wilko,
I am sure the chances of you getting this are slim at best. It is a thank you. Last year I was diagnosed with a Thymic Carcinoma the size of a grapefruit, had an operation, radiotherapy and was given 6 months to live. That time ended 28th July.
I am thriving not surviving.
I used to come down to The Kursal and Canvey, where I worked, to watch you in the early days ...still an enormous fan. Was in the front row at Glastonbury last year...... Fuck me Norman has still got it as well!!
I eagerly ordered the Ecstasy of Wilko from Amazon but was thrilled when the dear old BBC played it. I could only watch 10 mins on catch up last night as I got too emotional. Your words echoed mine almost exactly. I called my tumour Bob by the way after the character Bob in *Blackadder* who Lord Flashheart always fucked .... hence I was going to fuck Bob. Although losing a lung, fibrosis in the good one and a dodgy heart from the radiotherapy, I am still smiling and living every moment in the now. My book on this journey is called *Breaking Bob* and will be out just after Xmas.
You helped me so much in the dark days and I wanted to say

thank you, thank you, thank you, for helping me cope. I try to do the same to others...a positive butterfly effect.

I have a radio show in Coventry and would love it if you could spare 5 mins on the phone one day to let me say thank you publicly and give some hope to others battling as we have.

Sir you are a legend and you have my full fucking respect.

My number is 075** ******

May your days be beautiful

Namaste

Pillage

Much to my shock Mike said: "Wait until after the gig and I'll introduce you to him." I was in absolute shock. As soon as the concert ended mighty Ken and I were led into the underground recesses of the assembly rooms and told to wait. Two minutes later we were sitting in his dressing room.

They say never meet your heroes....utter balderdash. Wilko was a warm, generously spirited and beautiful man. I was expecting to shake his hand, get a pic and be ushered out. Forty minutes later we were still chatting. I spoke as honestly and from my heart as I have ever about our mutual fight and the similarities of experience that we had both encountered. When I explained just how much he had helped me he looked as if he had tears in his eyes. We hugged. We showed each other our scars and hugged magnificently again. However, the two incidents of note are as follows and in truth will stay with me until I die. The first was, he saw I had bought his biography and he kindly offered to autograph it. When he handed it back he had written his phone number and address and asked me to keep in touch, maybe even meet up when this book is finished. I was so touched.

The finale though still makes me laugh to this day and is a constant source of joy. He asked me about where the name Bob came from. I explained in full and he laughed out loud. It appears that Rik Mayall was a very close personal friend and that his character Rik - The Peoples Poet in The Young Ones (even the haircut) was entirely based on Wilko. How cool was this? Unbelievable.

As those of you will have noted the Flashheart WOOF has accompanied me throughout my illness as a term of rebellion and resistance against the fucking cancer. Many of you have in fact shared the Woof a million times on social media.

It has been a HUGE part of the fight.

Wilko then got up with a wry smile lifted his shirt to expose his scar. Bade me to do the same, put his hands on his hips and we WOOFED fucking magnificently at each other in true Flashheart Style. One of the most surreal and beautiful moments of my life. We laughed, hugged again and I left.

As a small addendum, I sent him The Pillage Party T-shirt with his name on the back as a small gift to say thank you for his time. Two days later I unexpectedly got a picture of him wearing it. Again, what a wonderful memory.

Wilko has two wonderful and very differing books out at present. One is called Looking Back at Me. *A brilliant book on his life through amazing pictures, especially the* Feelgood *Years. The second is more intimate* Don't Leave Me Here, My Life, *which is beautifully written and deals with his cancer. Both hugely recommended.*

What a fitting end to this tome. If you are reading this as a cancer survivor then I salute thee with awesomeness. We know the enormity of the battles you have fought and just how fucking incredible you are just to be here and alive through everything you have had to endure.

I metaphorically came out of the cancer closet and shared the entire journey. That was MY coping mechanism. For others, a secret and private battle takes place. It matters not; it's YOUR JOURNEY and YOURS ALONE to travel. As friends and family of people like us please remember this. No one can live it apart from the person who is ill. NO-ONE. Just be there when needed and do not judge our decisions as they are ours alone to make.

We do not want to be defined as a cancer sufferer but realize what a fucking HUGE deal it is and we need that Whooping and Woofing when we win those small battles by those surrounding us. So instead of waiting for us to die and then talking about us in marvelous tones about just what a great person we were, bloody well tell us now, tell us the good things and tell us you love us. It's better now when we can enjoy it I promise you.

May I thank all of you for reading my ramblings and please remember that cancer may not necessarily be the death sentence we believe it is at the time of knowing. The most important weapon you have in this war is the power of your own mind. That is the key. If you let the bastard take a hold you will lose your will to just fight and fight and fight to the best ability that you can. That will keep you alive my friends. NEVER FUCKING EVER give up.

In the appendix I will share the many potions and powders I have used and what I believe has kept me alive. As well as the

mindset and hope that maybe this book will give you a small insight into the whole cancer experience through the eyes of someone who just wouldn't fucking die.
Much love
Tata
Namaste, Pillagius Maximus xx

Appendix 1

Here is a list of all the supplements I take even to this day. I 100% believe that somewhere in this mad concoction lies the answer as to why I am still alive.

"ALIVE" MULTIVITAMINS
ACAI
ACIDOPHILIS
ARTECIN
ARTEMISIAN EXTRACT
ARTESINATE
AVOCADO OIL
B COMPLEX B10 FORMULA
B17 NOVO DARLIN BITTER APRICOT KERNELS
B6/CIDER VINEGAR
BARLEY GRASS
BEE PROPOLIS
BEETROOT EXTRACT
BEST ARTEMISIN
BEST NONI CONCENTRATE
BETA CAROTINE
BLACK RASPBERRY T10-
BLACK SEED OIL
BLACK WALNUT HUSKS
BROCCOLI EXTRACT
BROMOLAIN
BUFFERED VIT C
CALCIUM/MAGNESIUM
CALCIUM
CANNABIS OIL
CARNITINE

CATS CLAW
CHOLINE
CIDER VINGEAR + LECITHIN + VIT B6 + KELP
CO-ENZYME 10
DANDELION ROOT
DIGESTIVE ENZYME
DRIBOSE
ESSIAC VEG CAPSULES
FAB8
FRANKINSENSE (Yellow)
FULL-SPECTRUM WOODWOOD
GINGER ROOT EXTRACT
GINGKO BILBOA
GLUTOTHIONE REDUCED
GRAPESEED EXTRACT
GRAVIOLA
GREEN TEA EXTRACT
HEMP OIL
IP6 - INOSITOL/HEXA PHOSPHATE
IRON
KELP/IODINE
KOREAN GINSENG
KRILL OIL
L-ARGININE/L-ORTHININE-LYSINE
LEPICOL PRE/POST COMPLEX
LIVER GI DETOX
LYCOPENE
MACA ROOT EXTRACT
MERINGA OLIFERA
MILK THISTLE
MISETLETOE TINCTURE

BREAKING BOB

MIXED ASCORBATE POWDER
NAC (N-ACETYL-CUSTEINE)
OLIVE LEAF EXTRACT
ORNAGIC CHROLELLA TABLETS
PHOUR SALTS
POLYPHENOL NUTRIENTS
POMI T
PROBIOTIC PLUS
PROPOLIS
PUKKA VITALISE
REISHI MUSHROOM
RESVERTAROL
RHUBARB ROOT
SELENIUM
SERAPEPTASE 8,000 IU
SIBERIAN GINSENG
SODIUM BICARBONATE
SPIRULINA
STEVIA
SUPER ARTEMISIN
SUPERGARLIC
T10 FORMULA
THYME LEAF EXTRACT
TRIPLE MAGNESIUM COMPLEX
TUMERIC CAPSULES
TURKEY TAIL TINCTURE
URIDINE
VIT B COMPLEX, VIT B1, VIT B12
VIT D3/K2 MIX
VIT E
ZINC MIX

This is what everything looks like. I would be heard walking down the street long before anyone saw me.

Appendix 2

So here is a little life mantra I have put together ... my own Desiderata for my post cancer world.
Pillages Desiderata (with massive nod to Billy Connolly).

1   Treat people with the respect they deserve
2   Do stuff that nourishes your soul
3   Do whatever it takes to get to Glastonbury at least once in your lifetime
4   Spend time alone in thought
5   If you must lie about your age, do it in the other direction: tell people you're 65 and they'll think you look great
6   Do not be subservient to any man
7   Remember that life is actually quite simple
8   If you don't know how to meditate at least try to spend some time every day just sitting
9   Life is 100% about the people that you meet on the journey
10   Be passionate...it matters not what about
11   Play the didgeridoo
12   Sleep with somebody you like
13   Eat plenty of cake
14   Try to live in a place you like
15   Take the path less travelled
16   Always do a job you like
17   Never turn down an opportunity to shout, 'Fuck them all!' at the top of your voice
18   Avoid bigots of all descriptions
19   Open your mind, your heart and your soul
20   Learn to recognize kindred souls on the same path as you

21   Be kind and try to do random acts of kindness everyday
22   Never, ever give up
23   Read everyday
24   Avoid people who say they know the answer
25   Keep the company of people who are trying to understand the question
26   Have at least one cat
27   If you haven't heard a good rumour by 11:00am, start one
28   Play music often
29   If you write a book, be sure it has exactly seventy-six 'fucks' in it
30   Send Hieronymus Bosch prints to elderly relatives for Christmas
31   Use the word Namaste whenever you damn well feel like it
32   Remember the phrase Carpe Diem and seize the fucking day, EVERYDAY
33   DON'T PROCRASTINATE...time is shorter than you can ever believe
34   Spend time with the elderly as you will learn much from them
35   Share your dreams and listen to what other strive for in theirs
36   Stand up for what you truly believe in, whatever the cost to you
37   Believe in magyck and find some in your soul
38   Above all, do the hardest thing in the world and learn that it's OK to be you in all its fucked up glory and remember 'It's good to be alive!'

Appendix 3:

Filmography:
Dead Poets Society (1989) Film, Directed by: Weir P, USA, Touchstone Pictures and Silver Screen Partners IV
The Parrot Sketch (1969) Comedy Sketch. Written by: Cleese J & Chapman G – Monty Python

Bibliography:
Whitman, W., *O me, O life* (1900) Poem, Public Domain
Lynch, L., (2010). *The C Word.* London: Arrow

Discography:
Garvey, G., (2008) *One Day Like This* on *The Seldom Seen Kid* (Album) London, Fiction Records

Acknowledgements:

I could not possibly name every person who has been sharing the past two years with me ...there are far too many. But the following are whom I credit my life too. But I sincerely thank EVERY SINGLE PERSON who has contacted me, sent messages, phoned or visited me personally or on social media. The collective energy of you guys has been the very essence of life itself to me. Bows humbly to all.

Dr Tom Harper. Hadn't been for you I'd be dead.
Dr John Fullbrook. For the incredible levels of support throughout and for heading up the most amazing Medical Practice imaginable.
Mr Joseph Marzouk. Skilled surgeon and Bob slayer
Dr Mark Hocking. Tireless in his levels of support, help and fabulous oncologist
All the medical staff I have met especially at the Arden Centre in Coventry
Scott Caldwell and Russ Jarmesty for just being mates and haunting my dreams and not letting me ever give up.
Kevin and Jenni Mills for just being them.
Ric Lovett for moving heaven and earth for my re-birth !!
Mighty Ken and Pronoy for getting me to Glastonbury.
Eddie Quinn and Mikey Wright the best of men.
Mike Knight and Steph for always being there and never judging (at least to my face !!)
Wilko Johnson For just being fucking awesome.
Richard Barnes For being such a fabulous listener , making sense at times where there wasn't any and rugby host.
Richard Green for doing a fab job at the dojo.
Andy Haynes for evolving into the finest of Sifu's and people.
Mark Brown for teaching me the essence of bravery.

Nathan Hendry for being the most loyal and beautiful of friends.

Tony Bailey. Girth Brother and saver of sanity.

Lisa Lynch. For making me smile and cry often at the same time. You helped me more than you could know

Sarah Pillage. Your love and care saw me through this. You are a woman of substance, light and healing. Thank you for being you. Much love and respect.

I need to thank a few people who have helped me get this book to print. Firstly Courtney Neal for the initial transcribing of all the millions of Facebook posts. Kimberley Camp for her amazing job of getting the rest done in double quick time and of course Mrs. P, the cover designer.

And, of course, to all the people out there going through the awful experience of their own Bob.

I wish you all love, peace and life.

Namaste xxx